The Business Idea Factory

A World-Class System for Creating Successful Business Ideas

D1298685

Andrii Sedniev

The Business Idea Factory

A World-Class System for Creating Successful Business Ideas

Published by Andrii Sedniev

Copyright © 2019 by Andrii Sedniev

ISBN 978-1-07438-411-1

First printing, 2019

www.AndriiSedniev.com

PRINTED IN THE UNITED STATES OF AMERICA

Dedications

This book and my love are dedicated to Olena, my wife and partner, who makes every day in life worthwhile. Thank you for supporting me in every stage of development of *The Business Idea Factory* system and giving encouragement when I needed it the most. Without you, this book might never have been finished.

I also want to dedicate this book to all past students of the *The Business Idea Factory* system who, by their success, inspire me to become a better person every day.

Contents

Introduction

Imagine that you were born in the 16th century. Your occupation and future would be mostly predetermined by the family you were born into. If you wanted to become successful, you would have to be born into the family of a king, a bishop or a wealthy trader. Luckily those days are gone.

We live in the idea age. Companies succeed because of great ideas and go bankrupt because of lack of them. Some of the most successful companies such as Microsoft, Walmart, Apple and Honda became successful not because of the wealth and social status of the families their founders were born into, but because of the ideas behind them.

Imagine what your life might look like if you could improve the quantity and quality of business ideas that you generate, multiple times. You could create a business that would change the world. You could change the lives of millions of people and leave a mark in history. You could make each of your days more adventurous and interesting.

In 1968 George Land and Beth Jarman gave a test, used by NASA to measure the creativity of engineers and scientists, to 1,600 five-year-old kids. Later, they gave the same test to kids at the age of 10 and 15. The results showed that at the age of five, 98% of children demonstrate genius level of creativity; at the age of 10, about 30% of children demonstrate genius level of creativity, and at the age of 15, only 10%. The same test was given to a group of adults and among them only 2% showed genius level of creativity.

Children are extremely creative but when they begin going to school their creativity drops significantly. In school, children learn that there is only one answer for each question and are requested to conform to conventional social wisdoms The difference between geniuses and most of us is that they managed to not lose their childhood creativity.

The great news is that you can significantly improve your ability to generate successful business ideas. Over the last 10 years I have researched business idea generation techniques used by the world's best scientists, entrepreneurs, CEOs and innovators. I carefully collected and analyzed every small bit of wisdom that may increase the number and quality of business ideas that one can produce. As a result, the *Business Idea Factory* system was created which describes an extremely effective and easy-to-use process for creating successful business ideas.

I promise that if you apply the strategies described in this book daily, you will increase the number and quality of business ideas that you create multiple times. After my students and I began using this system, the number and quality of business ideas that we produced increased hundreds of times. Many people began new businesses after reading this book, significantly increased revenue in their existing businesses and became more successful. I promise that if you take the techniques described in this book seriously and begin implementing them today, your life will change for the better. There are few things that can bring as much joy and success in business as the moment when an excellent idea comes into your head. Are you ready to build your business idea factory? Let's begin.

Creative brain vs. analytical brain

Activate your super-fast brain

Numerous research studies were conducted to compare the performance of our right brain (subconscious mind) and left brain (conscious mind). The results confirmed that our creative right brain is at least 2 million times faster than our analytical left brain. The analytical left brain is responsible for judging, self-monitoring and internal dialogue. It prevents you from saying everything you think and doing everything you consider. The right brain is responsible for generating new creative ideas.

In his research at Johns Hopkins University, Charles Limb asked jazz musicians and rap artists to compose an improvisational piece of music. While they were playing, Charles measured the activity of different areas of the brain. During this creative improvisation, the part of the brain responsible for analytical thinking and judgment showed much lower activity.

The right brain is responsible for all activities that involve creativity and can process enormous amounts of information within seconds. The conscious mind is not only useless for generating business ideas but, in fact, blocks the subconscious mind from doing its work. To become world class at generating business ideas you need to learn how to turn your analytical brain off and let the subconscious mind think.

If you want to effectively generate business ideas, you need to avoid any activities that engage the left brain that blocks the subconscious mind. When you think about your task, remember 3 rules: no judging, no criticizing and no internal dialoguing.

Walt Disney strategy

Walt Disney was certainly one of the most creative people in the 20th century. With his skill of generating successful business ideas, he built one of the biggest media conglomerates in the world. Walt Disney created fantastical ideas that might have sounded crazy and unfeasible at first glance, then considered how to make these fantasies a reality and finally evaluated them. In the process of generating new ideas, Walt separated his thinking into 3 stages: Dreamer, Realist and Critic.

A Dreamer generates creative ideas. There are no limitations and your imagination can take you anywhere. Imagine that you have a magic wand and everything is possible. For the Dreamer, cats can fly, houses are made of ice cream, TVs have legs and dance. At this stage your goal is to create and write down as many ideas as possible and the crazier they are, the better. You will have multiple opportunities to judge your ideas later, but while being a Dreamer turn off your analytical left brain. Judging and evaluating block your creative subconscious mind.

The Realist answers the question, "How can I make this idea a reality?" At this stage, you decide how to adopt or modify the idea to make it practical for the market. Even if you decide to discard the idea later, you need to first ponder how to make it real and how it can be combined with your other ideas. Give each idea a chance to live before criticizing it.

As the Critic, you should identify potential flaws of the idea. Why might it not work? What potential problems and difficulties in implementation could your idea have? Most important for you is to begin judging and evaluating ideas only after you have been a Dreamer and Realist. The majority of people criticize their ideas at the Dreamer stage and not only block the idea generation process, but kill the ideas too early. Often the idea may sound crazy at the beginning, but with slight modification or in combination with other ideas may lead to a successful business.

In 1943 Edwin Land took a picture of his 3-year-old daughter. She asked, "Dad, why can't I see the picture that you have taken right away?" Edwin thought about how to make this idea a reality and in 4 years the first Polaroid camera was released. Had the daughter of Edwin Land known why pictures couldn't be made instantaneously or had Edwin discarded her idea instantly instead of first thinking about how to make it a reality, the world would never have seen Polaroid.

Whenever you think about ideas always separate dreaming and judging. These two processes don't get along well. This simple thinking strategy can have a dramatic impact on the quantity and quality of ideas that you generate.

I just need one big idea

If you asked me: "Andrii, can you say what events have influenced your life the most?" a conversation with James in New York's JFK Airport would be certainly one of the events I mention.

James was sitting next to me at the departure gate waiting for his flight to Charlotte and began a casual conversation. I learned that James had successfully sold several IT companies for more than $100M. However, what impressed me even more was that with all this money he was traveling in economy class and was dressed in a way that would never reveal that he is rich.

In the middle of the conversation I said, "You know, James, I truly envy your entrepreneurial gift. Since childhood I have dreamt about starting a company like Microsoft, but realized that I have no talent of generating great business ideas."

James smiled at me and said, "Really? How did you come to this conclusion?"

"Since childhood I wanted to become an entrepreneur but couldn't stumble upon a big business idea that could make me rich and famous like Bill Gates. A year ago I decided, 'I will lock myself in a room and will think until I come up with a big business idea or until I give up on becoming an entrepreneur.' For eighteen hours straight I was thinking and staring at the wall, thinking and staring at the ceiling, thinking and walking back and forth. I didn't come up with an outstanding business idea and gave up on my childhood dream."

"Andrii, you might not know this, but before Microsoft, Bill Gates created Traf-O-Data, a company that prepared reports for traffic engineers based on data from roadway traffic counters. This company didn't have big success but the experience was very valuable for creating Microsoft.

"When I became an entrepreneur with my first company I lost money, and my second company brought me less income per year than if I worked for minimum wage. But without the first 2 companies I would never have enough experience and knowledge to create the third company that I eventually sold for over $40M.

"Andrii, forget about a big idea. Your chances of creating it while staring at the wall are less than winning the lottery. Just begin implementing any of your business ideas and in the process many bigger ideas will come to you. Great ideas are created based on your life experiences and to get them you should be actively doing something."

This short conversation with James changed my attitude towards entrepreneurship. Had I not met James, I might still not have opened my own business and have joy from seeing how my students generate excellent business ideas daily and become successful.

When I talk to people I often hear, "Andrii, I envy your entrepreneurial gift. I'd like to start my own business but I don't have enough starting capital and a big business idea." I always say, "Just begin implementing today the best business ideas that you have with the starting capital that you have. In the process you will learn how to promote, how to sell, how to collaborate with other people, how to generate ideas and solve problems. Once you hit a really big business idea, you will have enough experience and resources to make it a success."

Exercise: A $100 hour

A $100 hour is one of my favorite exercises for generating business ideas. It will help you create many interesting ideas, some of which may bring enormous success.

Think for one hour about how you can make an extra $100. In this exercise you don't need to think about how to change the world, how to become a billionaire or how to create a steady stream of income. Your only goal is to generate as many ideas as possible of how you can earn an extra $100. That's it. After the completion of the exercise, pick the one idea that you like the most and make a commitment to implement it. After you implement this business idea you will know if it works, if you can scale it and if you can outsource some tasks.

The $100 hour technique is very easy and fun to do and it can bring your business enormous success. Your subconscious mind may be paralyzed by the thought, "I have to create a big business idea that will change my life," but it will eagerly generate business ideas that can bring an extra $100. Some of these ideas will become big, profitable and successful businesses. The $100 hour technique will bring you many interesting ideas, but only under the condition that you do it regularly. When you are ironing, jogging, gardening, waiting in line or feeling bored during a corporate meeting, it's a wonderful time for the $100 hour.

Programming the mind

During the day

One day I went to the stadium near my house to jog and after several rounds a question popped up in my head: "Why are there days when I create hundreds of excellent ideas and there are other days when I create zero ideas?" In a few minutes I realized why this happens, and thought, "Thank you, universe, for sending me this insight. I see how it can make a huge impact on my ability to generate successful business ideas. This is perhaps the biggest gift I ever received."

Once you learn the difference between generating hundreds of excellent ideas per day and no ideas at all you may think, "Hey, Andrii, it's logical and obvious." However, this simple insight can increase the number and quality of ideas you produce many times. In fact, if you take this insight seriously people will think that you are a genius.

The day when you create hundreds of ideas, you ask yourself questions and give your brain problems to think about: "How do I draw more visitors to my company website? What other products can my company produce? How do I increase sales?" The day you create zero ideas, is the day you don't give your brain any tasks. If you don't know what ideas you need, your brain simply remains idle and your subconscious mind doesn't do any work.

In the 1960s my grandmother saw a computer for the first time in her life. Her brother, Yuriy, brought her to the computer lab of the university where he worked and said, "Alina, this is one of the most powerful computers of our time. There are less than 10 such computers in the Ukraine." My grandma asked, "It's almost 1 a.m. Why are there people still working here?"

"You see, Alina, there is only one computer in the entire university and it's extremely expensive and powerful. Professors and PhD students are sharing time on it and it's never idle."

If you want to become a world-class business ideas creator, your brain should also never be idle. No, I don't mean that you need to work hard or be thinking for hours about your problems. You just need to decide which ideas you need and give your brain tasks. If you just think about several problems for, say, 15 minutes a day, it will be enough to set a program for your subconscious mind. It will process millions of combinations while you exercise at the gym, have lunch with your friend or while you sleep. Eventually you will get many new ideas in the form of insight or a creativity spark.

Realizing which ideas you need and giving your brain tasks daily is the difference between creating thousands of ideas and no ideas at all. It is also the difference between enormous success in business and no success at all.

Before you sleep

Several years ago I was an audience member during a corporate presentation. I remember a speaker saying, "If you want to work at my company, you may expect to work about

16 hours per day." Somebody in the audience asked, "Does this time include sleep?" And the audience burst out in laughter.

In fact, sleep time can be the most productive time for generating business ideas if you know how to use it properly. While you sleep the subconscious mind works even more productively than during the day because it's not blocked by the analytical brain. However, it will generate outstanding business ideas for you only if you activate it properly.

You may ask, "Andrii, how can I activate my subconscious mind before I go to bed?" While I was a high school student I often worked on solving math problems until late. When I got stuck on a particular problem and got tired, I went to bed. Very often, when I woke up in the morning, I had an idea of how to proceed with solving the problem.

When you think about your task just before sleep, it's the same as telling your subconscious, "Here is a question I need an answer for. Please generate ideas for me." Your subconscious gets the message and works the entire night while you sleep. Once you think about the task again in the morning you will get valuable ideas. The subconscious doesn't speak our language, but conveys ideas through intuition or gut feeling. Don't try to understand where the ideas come from. It's impossible. Just expect them to come. Trust your subconscious mind and appreciate what it does for you.

Glass of water technique

"Glass of water" is one of the most effective and powerful creativity techniques that exist. It's extremely easy to use, however it can make miracles with your ability to generate excellent ideas while you sleep. The author of this technique is Jose Silva, who became famous worldwide by developing a complex of psychological exercises called the Silva Method.

Take a water glass and fill it with clean but not boiled water. With both hands, take the glass, close your eyes and look upward at a 45-degree angle. Formulate a task that you need to solve as a question. Then, drink half of the glass of water while thinking, "This is all I need to find the solution to the problem I have in mind."

Open your eyes. Put the glass of water near the bed and go to sleep without talking to anyone. In most cases you will receive an answer while you sleep in the form of a hint, insight or partial idea. Once you wake up, immediately write down all ideas, memories and thoughts that come to mind. Drink the second half-glass of water and thank your subconscious for the work that was done.

If you didn't get a satisfying answer, close your eyes, look slightly upward and drink the second half-glass of water while thinking, "This is all I need to find the solution to the problem I have in mind." The idea for the problem's solution will come to you during the day. And one more thing, believe that ideas will come to you.

You might think, "Can I use a cup instead of the glass? Can I say a different phrase while drinking the water? Can I do this technique without water at all?" This technique works most effectively if you don't change anything. It's critical to use a glass, it's critical what you say, and it's critical that you expect ideas to come. Follow these instructions as a ritual. It works in 100% of the cases for me, it works for thousands of people who tried it, and it will work for you.

Genius inventors realize that many breakthrough ideas came to them while they slept. If you need a creative business idea, don't sit at your desk until late. The subconscious processes millions of thoughts while you are not consciously thinking about the problem and sleep is a time when it works best. Just go to bed, let your subconscious know what problem needs to be solved and in the morning write down all thoughts that come to your head.

Set a task

Ask the right question

Before generating business ideas you need to decide which problem or task you will think about. Asking the right question is extremely critical because it will determine the direction in which your brain will think and the type of ideas your subconscious will generate. For example, if you lived in the 19th century and asked: "How can I create faster horses?" you might have gotten ideas about how to create a breed of faster horses or develop an effective training for horses. However, if you asked, "How can I get people from point A to point B faster?" you might have invented a car, a train or a plane.

Several questions are better than one

You may ask, "Andrii, it's easy to know which question to ask looking into the past. How can I know which question is right for my problem that hasn't been solved yet?" Well, the more questions you ask, the higher the chance of finding a right question and generating a successful idea.

Spend 10 minutes thinking about your problem. Quickly write down at least 10 different versions of the question you want to answer. Do not judge or evaluate questions so as to not activate the analytical left brain. Your goal is to create as many questions as possible no matter how crazy or unreasonable. Pick several questions that will allow you to look at the problem from different perspectives. If while working on the problem you think in several different directions, your chances of finding a successful business idea will be higher.

For example, if you want to answer the question, "How can I increase sales of the washing machines that my plant produces?" you may express the same concept in the following ways: "How can I sell more than one washing machine to each customer?" "What new products can I sell?" "How can the plant increase the revenue?" "How can I sell washing machines not just to households, but also to companies?" "How can I effectively promote the washing machines?" "How can I increase the quality of my washing machines?" "How can I hire or train the most qualified sales representatives in the market?" Thinking about each of these questions may bring you to the solution that the first question won't.

Sometimes you don't create the successful business idea simply because you asked the wrong question. No matter how experienced or talented you are, you won't arrive at the right question every single time. If while thinking on your problem you change questions occasionally, it will increase the quality and quantity of successful ideas that you create. Always remember that the direction in which you think may predetermine your ideas.

Questions that bring results

Your questions should be specific and action oriented for your subconscious to generate excellent ideas. For example, instead of "Why don't I have money to buy a new car?" ask "How can I earn enough money to buy a new Honda Civic?" After asking a first question, your subconscious mind may answer without thinking, "Because you don't earn enough to buy a car." If you ask a second question in the example, your subconscious will suggest specific strategies for earning more money. It will also know how much money you need exactly and suggest the ideas accordingly.

After becoming CEO of Ford, Donald Petersen replaced sophisticated rules that a design center had to follow for creating new cars with a simple guideline: "Design something that you would be proud to park in your driveway." This change in direction for the brains of Ford engineers allowed them to design the highly successful Ford Taurus.

Toyota management asked employees, "Please give ideas of how the company can become more productive" and received very few ideas. Later they reworded the question to "How can you make your job easier?" and received an enormous amount of valuable ideas.

Edward Jenner invented the smallpox vaccine by changing a question from "How can we prevent smallpox?" to "Why don't milkmaids get smallpox?"

In many instances, if you can't create a successful business idea, it means that you simply asked a wrong question. When you are stuck and don't make any progress, spend some time restating a question. By describing a problem in several different ways, you will look at it from different perspectives and generate different ideas. Even a tiny change in the question that you ask yourself may dramatically improve the quantity and quality of business ideas that your subconscious will generate.

Pyramid of problems

Change abstraction level of the question

Each question you ask has an abstraction level. By decreasing or increasing the abstraction level, you may stimulate your brain to come up with new ideas you haven't ever thought about. An excellent technique for changing an abstraction level of the problem is the "5 Whys" technique. For example, if you want to create ideas that will answer the question, "How can I increase sales of the T54 model of washing machines that my plant produces?" ask "Why" 5 times.

Step 1: Why do you want to sell more T54 washing machines? "Because I want to sell more washing machines overall."

Step 2: Why do you want to sell more washing machines? "Because I want to improve overall sales."

Step 3: Why do you want to improve overall sales? "To make my business more profitable."

Step 4: Why do you want to make your business more profitable? "To increase my personal wealth."

Step 5: Why do you want to increase your personal wealth? "To earn enough money, so that I can work less and spend more time with my family."

Answering each of the following questions will allow you to generate ideas that will solve your problem: "How can I work less and spend more time with my family?" "How can I increase my personal wealth?" "How can I make my business more profitable?" "How can I increase overall sales?" "How can I sell more washing machines?" and "How can I sell more T54s?" Once you change an abstraction level to a higher or a lower one, you may come up with ideas that you weren't able to create with a previous question. For example, if you phrase a question as "How can I increase overall sales?" you may come up with an idea to begin producing laundry dryers in addition to washing machines. And if you phrase the question as "How can I work less and spend more time with my family?" you can come up with an idea to delegate some tasks to an assistant or to optimize your work processes.

Changing the abstraction level of your question will change the direction of your thinking. Sometimes you might think, "Oh, it's a dead end. I just can't come up with a really good idea." However, the real problem is not that you don't get appropriate ideas, but that you directed your thinking to the wrong path. Change an abstraction level of the problem or reword a question and completely different ideas will come to your head. Be sure that one of them will be a perfect solution for your task.

Break a problem into pieces

Many years ago I asked a serial entrepreneur, multimillionaire and exceptional problem-solver, "Jason, imagine that you want to launch a new business. How would you decide which actions to take first?"

"Andrii, if I wake up in the morning and decide to become a chocolate producer, I break this complex task into several simpler ones: 'How can I produce tasty chocolates?' and 'How can I sell many chocolates?'

"Each of these problems I split into several even smaller problems. 'How can I produce tasty chocolates?' may be split into: 'How do I get a recipe for tasty chocolate?' and 'How do I outsource production of my chocolate?' The task, 'How can I sell many chocolates?' may be split into: 'How can I sell chocolates through supermarkets?' and 'How can I promote chocolates through media?'

"All tasks get split into smaller tasks until they get so small that by thinking about them, I can come to specific actions that need to be taken.

"I use this strategy every day for solving complex business tasks. Andrii, if you want to solve a complex problem, just build a pyramid from smaller problems and you will be able to solve tasks that seem unsolvable from the first glance."

Once you create an idea of what business you want to be in, the process of generating business ideas only begins. You will need to create thousands of smaller ideas that will answer questions about how to implement each element of the business such as: promotion, hiring talent, outsourcing product development, marketing or sales. Practice changing the abstraction level of your questions and you will be easily able to switch between strategic tasks and everyday implementation tasks. Practice splitting big tasks into smaller ones and there will be no problem for which you can't create a brilliant solution. Remember that businesses become great one idea at a time.

Imagine that you work for minimum wage and you have a childhood dream to travel around the world for 6 months on a luxurious yacht. You ask yourself, "How can I earn

$200,000 to buy a luxurious yacht for my trip?" After brainstorming for a week, you come to a conclusion, "With my current salary there is no way I can make my childhood dream a reality." Let's see how applying techniques from this section can make a trip possible within a very short period of time.

Firstly, let's reword this question to: "How can I spend 6 months on a luxurious yacht?" and "How can I travel on a luxurious yacht for cheap?" The answer to these questions can be, "I can rent a yacht for 6 months. It will cost only $20,000" and "I can share the expenses with 9 people who also want to travel the world on the luxurious yacht."

Secondly, let's break the task into 2 smaller pieces: "Where can I find 9 people who want to travel on a luxurious yacht?" and "How can I save $2,000 for the trip?" Both of these tasks are much more feasible than earning $200,000 but lead you to fulfillment of the same dream.

Albert Einstein said, "The formulation of a problem is often more essential than its solution, which may be merely a matter of mathematical or experimental skills. To raise new questions ... requires creative imagination and makes real advances."

If you can't find a solution for a business task, it's very likely that you are simply asking the wrong question. Change the questions you are thinking about, change the abstraction level and break big problems into pieces. If you apply these techniques regularly, you will soon realize that you can solve problems of any difficulty.

Think and Rest

Think and Rest technique

During a summer between high school and university, I learned that a Cisco Certified Internetwork Expert (CCIE) is the most prestigious IT certification in the world. My dad said, "Andrii, there are only a few dozen CCIEs in all of the ex-USSR countries, they earn six-figure salaries and companies fight to get them hired." I set the goal, "I will become a CCIE no matter what."

In 2 years, I passed the CCIE written exam and the only thing that separated me and my dream was the CCIE lab part of the exam. To pass it you needed to configure a rack with 16 network devices according to the scenario presented.

I asked several Internetwork Experts, "How did you manage to get access to equipment worth $20,000 to prepare for the CCIE lab exam?" and received two types of answers: "The company I worked at provided access to the equipment" and "I spent my own money on access to a remote rack with equipment."

In 3 months I realized, "Not a single company in the Ukraine wants to hire an 18-year-old part-time for enough money to prepare for the CCIE lab." A friend who worked for the Cisco local distributor arranged for me to use some equipment, but after only 2 days of my practice it had been sold. I thought, "I tried all approaches that worked for others in the past and failed. It's a dead end."

In my case there was no reasonable way to get access to the expensive equipment. One day I visited the websites of all the companies that dealt with Cisco certifications, found email addresses of the CEOs and wrote the following letter, "Hi, I am 18 years old and have already passed the written part of the CCIE exam. If you can provide me access to the equipment necessary to prepare for the CCIE lab part of the exam, I am ready to do any work for you in exchange. You will also be able to say in your promotional materials that the youngest CCIE in Europe has gained the certification with the help of your company."

Looking back, I think that sending out that email was crazy, unreasonable and unprofessional. Who knew that one company would offer me a job to help improve their testing materials in exchange for money, and another would offer to have me write a brochure in exchange for equipment access during the time slots that were not sold to paying customers.

At 19, I passed the lab exam in Brussels, became the youngest CCIE in Europe and received a job offer from the Cisco office in the Ukraine. I attribute this success to an unconventional idea that allowed me to get access to expensive equipment and I attribute this idea to the Think and Rest technique that allowed me to generate it.

If you asked me, "Andrii, what is the most effective thinking strategy to produce high-quality business ideas?" I would certainly say, "Of, course Think and Rest." Think and Rest is an incredibly effective thinking technique that will allow you to produce successful business ideas with little effort.

Firstly, think about the problem you want to solve as hard as you can for 30 minutes, 60 minutes or several hours and write down all the ideas that come to your head, no matter how crazy. During this initial thinking stage you not only generate ideas but also let your subconscious mind know which ideas you need. If your problem is simple, you may find a good solution already during this initial brainstorming session, but if you didn't find an appropriate solution within the first several hours, forget about your problem completely and get back to your everyday life.

Secondly, after you stop thinking about the problem consciously, the subconscious will continue thinking about it 24/7. Your super-fast creative mind will process millions of thoughts and give you ideas while you are on a walk, taking a shower or sleeping. The subconscious mind is responsible for most original and successful ideas that you create. Once the subconscious generates an idea for you, write it down no matter where you are and what time of the day it is.

Finally, think about your task occasionally for 2 to 5 minutes. During this time you will not only generate fresh ideas but will also reactivate your creative mind and make it think intensively while you are not consciously thinking about the problem.

The Think and Rest technique will help you generate successful business ideas in 100% of cases. If after using this technique a great idea didn't come to you, it means that either not enough time has passed or that you don't have enough raw materials to create an idea from and need to do more research.

Think and Rest is a strategy that most effectively activates the thinking process in the brain. To become as effective at generating successful business ideas as possible, use Think and Rest consciously. The best innovators and thinkers in the world use this strategy daily.

Incubation period

If after a period of intense thinking you didn't generate an excellent idea, forget about the problem and switch to a completely different activity. Your analytical brain has set a program for your creative brain, which will continue thinking about the problem 24/7 in the back of your mind.

During the time when you don't consciously focus on the problem, the creative brain makes random connections between millions of thoughts in the back of your mind, and once it sees that one of the connections seems interesting it says, "Eureka! Here is an interesting idea." The more time your subconscious mind thinks about a problem, the more connections it makes and the higher the probability that a successful business idea will be generated.

A majority of scientists and entrepreneurs reported that they got their best ideas and insights while not actively thinking about the problem. The best ideas come when you forget about the problem and least expect them: while traveling, shaving, taking a shower, standing in line, jogging, talking to a friend, watching a play at the theater or sleeping.

When after an initial brainstorming session the flow of ideas dries up, get back to your everyday life. To keep the creative brain active, let it know that you still need ideas by occasionally thinking about the problem for few minutes from time to time. Great innovators are producing successful business ideas not because they work harder than others, but because they use an effective thinking process. Although the work that the subconscious mind does during the incubation period is invisible, it is the most essential part of this process.

C.G. Suits, the legendary Chief Scientist at General Electric, said: "All the discoveries in research laboratories came as hunches during a period of relaxation, following a period of intensive thinking and fact gathering."

Bertrand Russell, the British logician and mathematician, said: "I have found, for example, that if I have to write upon some rather difficult topic, the best plan is to think about it with very great intensity – the greatest intensity of which I am capable – for a few hours or days, and at the end of that time give orders, so to speak (to my subconscious mind) that the work is to proceed underground. After some months I return consciously to the topic and find that the work has been done."

When Carl Sagan, the American astronomer, got stuck on one project he moved to another one, allowing his subconscious to do the work. He wrote: "When you come back, you find to your amazement, nine times out of ten, that you have solved your problem – or your unconscious has – without you even knowing it."

Think about different problems simultaneously

Many years ago at the age of 14 I was sitting in a room full of tenth-graders waiting for a math competition to begin. If you were in the room with me you would have heard the lady say: "You will have 4 hours to solve 4 problems. I will collect your papers promptly at the end of the contest. Now you can turn over your sheets with problem descriptions and begin. Good luck!"

After 60 minutes of thinking about the first problem, I thought, "I still haven't made any progress. If I spend as much time on all the other problems and make as much progress, I will definitely lose the competition. Let's see what the other problems are like."

I spent 10 minutes on problem number 2, made a little bit of progress, got stuck and moved on to problem number 3. After 20 minutes, I solved it. I thought, "Wow! Let's see what I can do with problem number 4." In 10 minutes after having thought about problem 4, I got stuck and moved back to problem number 1. After 15 minutes of thinking I made some more progress, got stuck again and moved to problem number 2. In 25 minutes I finally solved problem number 2. I was switching between the remaining problems over and over again until the end of the contest, and by the time the lady was collecting the papers I had solved 3 problems.

I became the second-place winner and received the right to represent my city at the country level math competition. But perhaps the most valuable prize I received was an invaluable lesson that helped me to generate ideas more effectively not only at school but also in adult life. "If you switch between problems, your subconscious will think about them simultaneously and your productivity at producing ideas will increase several times."

The creativity researcher Mihaly Csikszentmihalyi interviewed 96 exceptional scientists, artists and writers and realized that all of them worked on more than one project at a time. If you switch between several problems, your subconscious will think about all of them in the back of your mind while you work, rest and sleep, and you will generate many more great ideas at the same time. Working on several problems simultaneously is one of the most powerful creativity techniques and will significantly increase productivity of your subconscious mind during the incubation period.

Think in pictures

When my wife, Olena, began learning English, I realized that she speaks extremely slowly. I asked, "Olena, why is it when you want to say something you first make a huge pause and then slowly say one word after another?"

"Well, I first decide what I want to say in Russian, translate a sentence into English and then say it aloud."

"Olena, do you know how children learn to speak? A mother shows an orange to a child and says, 'It is orange.' Then she points at the house and says, 'It's a house.' After a while, a child associates in his or her mind a picture of an orange with the word 'orange' and a picture of the house with the word 'house.' If you want to speak quickly, you need to associate pictures of the objects and actions directly with English words and avoid making a translation in your mind. An analytical brain is responsible for translating and it significantly slows down a process of turning a thought into a sentence."

The same happens in your thinking about business ideas. If you try to talk to yourself or think using words, the conscious brain is activated, your thinking slows down millions of times and your chances of creating interesting ideas become very slim.

Albert Einstein, Thomas Edison and Henry Ford left enormous amounts of diagrams and pictures in their notebooks. One of the reasons why they were extremely successful idea creators was their habit of thinking visually. Albert Einstein said that he rarely thought in words. Thoughts came to him in images and only then did he express them with words and formulas.

Imagine a "car" and a "soap." Now, create several combinations of these objects to generate new ideas. You might say, "A soap that is in the form of a car, a car seat that is in the form of a soap, car washing using soap, a car that uses soap instead of fuel." But before you say all these ideas you may first imagine them in your head.

Remember that your super-fast subconscious mind thinks using pictures, and if you want to be effective at generating business ideas, you should think using pictures rather than words. Great ideas are first created as images in your head and only then described using words.

Quantity over quality of ideas

Avoid making decisions based on past experience

While studying at Yale University, Fred Smith wrote a paper in which he described a concept of Federal Express. His management professor gave him a "C" for the project and said, "The concept is interesting and well-formed, but in order to earn better than a 'C', the idea must be feasible." Once Fred founded FedEx, almost every delivery expert in the United States predicted that his company would fail based on their experience in the industry. They said that no one would pay a premium price for speed and reliability.

We are used to making decisions based on our past experience because in the majority of situations it's reasonable and helps avoid making the same mistake twice. If, however, you take into consideration only what worked in the past, you may come to the same old ideas. If you want to create successful business ideas, you need to tell the world what will work in the future, not what worked in the past.

Several years ago while studying how the brain works, I stumbled upon a very interesting statistic that said, "When you do kickboxing, your body burns about 10 calories per minute; when you walk, your body burns about 4 calories per minute; the brain on its own burns only about one tenth of a calorie per minute. However, when you actively think, the brain burns 1.5 calories per minute." Taking into account that the brain makes up only 2 percent of the body weight, that's a huge amount of energy!

Your brain always tries to conserve as much energy as possible. Once you begin thinking about any task, the brain quickly scans memory for past experiences and in a few seconds says: "Here is a solution." You say, "Hey, brain, I don't like this one. Give me another one." The brain looks into the past experiences and again in a few seconds says, "Here is a solution." Unfortunately, these solutions are often obvious and of little value for making a business successful.

Tell your friends, "Please write down a list of 20 animals." At the beginning, they will most probably list such animals as "cat," "dog," "bear" or "lion." These animals are freshest in your friends' memory, because they often see them on the street, in the zoo, on TV or in advertisements. At the end of the list there will be more rare animals such as "puma," "sloth" or "guinea pig."

Research shows that we recall common objects faster than less typical ones. Research also shows that when thinking about a problem, the brain tends to give most typical solutions based on past experience faster than original and creative solutions.

Your brain will avoid thinking really hard until it runs out of quick solutions based on your experience of what worked in the past. The only way to make the brain think hard and produce world-class ideas is to make it generate a lot of ideas.

The greatest innovators know this and when they think on a problem they are never satisfied with the first or second solution that comes to their head. They generate all the ideas they can and then pick the most promising ones. Einstein was once asked how his thinking was different from the thinking of the average person. He said, "When searching for a needle in a haystack, other people quit when they find a needle. I look for what other needles might be in the haystack."

Quantity equals quality

Imagine that you want to solve a particular problem and need one perfect solution. Many people would say, "Yeah, I will think until I find the perfect solution. Once I find it, I will stop thinking." Although this approach seems intuitive, it rarely works. Why? Let's review the thinking strategies of the left and right brain.

The left brain looks for one and the best solution for the problem. In everyday life, we use the left brain in a majority of cases and it gives us a good answer. You ask, "Which route should I choose to get to work? Is this coat expensive? In what year did the Second World War begin?" The left brain quickly looks at what worked in the past and answers, "Here is your best answer." We are so used to using the logical left brain every day that we try to use it even when we need a creative new solution. Unfortunately, the logical brain is not only useless for generating creative ideas, but is even harmful because it blocks the creative right brain.

The right brain is millions of times faster than the left logical brain and is responsible for generating creative and original ideas. The creative brain looks for many solutions for the same problem. Even though you may eventually implement only one solution, during the idea generation stage think about all possible and impossible solutions. The more ideas you create, the better your final solution will be.

Professor Dean Keith decided to explore the relationship between the quantity and quality of ideas. He studied the work of hundreds of the most creative scientists and made a very interesting discovery. The best scientists created more successful ideas than the mediocre ones. However, the best scientists also created many more bad ideas than the mediocre scientists.

The vast majority of papers written by the world's most famous scientists were never cited. A small percentage of them received a little over 100 citations and only several papers had an incredible impact on the world.

Professor Keith has done the same study with composers and other fine artists and found that the more bad ideas a composer, a scientist or an artist generated, the more successful ideas he or she had.

Thomas Edison filed over 2,000 patents, but the majority of them didn't make him a cent. Albert Einstein published over 300 scientific papers, but the majority of them are not cited by other scientists. Pablo Picasso created more than 20,000 pieces of art, but most of them are not presented at the best art exhibitions. There is a direct correlation between quantity and quality of ideas. The majority of ideas that the best ideas creators generate are bad, some of them are average and very few are genius. These few genius ideas make the best creators enormously successful.

Nature creates multiple species through blind trial and error and lets the process of natural selection decide which species survive. In nature, 95% of new species fail and die. Those species that survive, thrive and become part of the world's ecosystem. As an ideas generator, you need to generate a large quantity of ideas and give them a chance to live. A few of these ideas will survive and make your business incredibly successful. The more ideas you generate the more likely one of them will be a treasure. To become a world-class ideas creator, remember the most important equation in creativity: quantity equals quality.

Set ideas quota

Several years ago, I conducted a workshop, at a famous international company, about generating business ideas. I split the participants into groups and gave them a task, "Please come up with 100 applications of the brick. Your ideas can be crazy or unrealistic, but by all means meet the quantity requirement. You have 30 minutes, go!"

If you received such a task, at first you would quickly write down applications of the brick from your past experience. For example, "A brick can be used for building a house or a brick can be used as a weapon." In a few minutes the typical applications of the brick you can recall from your past experience end and this is the time when the brain begins really thinking.

For example, the ideas you might have will be something like, "A brick can be used as a musical instrument, as a toy and as a fan." You will realize that indeed creative and valuable ideas come after you have exhausted the most obvious ideas from your memory and lie somewhere between number 80 and number 100.

After the exercise with a brick, I gave participants another task, "Please come up with 200 headlines for the upcoming advertising campaign of the company's product. Your ideas can be crazy or unrealistic, but by all means meet the quantity requirement. You have 60 minutes, go!" If you are curious to know how the workshop participants finished the task, I will tell you. All groups came up with more than 200 ideas. Some of the ideas were extremely interesting and the company implemented one of them.

During a brainstorming session, set a goal to generate a large quantity of ideas within a short period of time. Put your internal critic on hold and let your imagination generate enough ideas, no matter how crazy, silly or unrealistic, to meet the quota. The first third of ideas will be old ideas from past experience, the second half will be more interesting ideas and the final third will most likely have exceptional ideas that will make your business successful. The ideas quota technique forces the creative brain to think, generate a large quantity of ideas, and later select the most promising among them.

The takeaway message from this section can be excellently summarized by the words of the international design firm IDEO founder David Kelley: "If you're forced to come up with ten things, it's the clichéd things that you have off the top of your head. But if you have to come up with a hundred, it forces you to go beyond the clichés."

Set constraints and think inside the box

One Monday when I was 12 years old, a teacher gave us homework. She said, "Please write an essay on any topic." In 3 days, my friend Max went to the teacher and said, "I was thinking hard for hours, but still don't have any ideas. I can't write even one line." The teacher asked, "Max, where do you live?" He said, "I live across the street from the theater." The teacher said, "Well, please write an essay about the left wing of the theater in front of your house." Max went home and wrote a 10-page essay in the afternoon. His essay was the best in class. Now Max is a director at an international creative agency and generating ideas is his everyday work.

In creativity there is nothing more paralyzing than the task to create anything you want with all the resources you need. Suppose you say, "I want to generate any business ideas. I have an unlimited amount of time and money for the project." That just kills creativity and you will be very unlikely to generate really good ideas. However, if you define how many ideas you want to generate, set a deadline, limit the budget for the project, and describe a task for your subconscious as specifically as possible, you will generate many outstanding ideas, some of which will eventually become successful businesses. Well-defined problems with a deadline, ideas quota and resources limitation have much more chance of being solved creatively.

Don't assume fake constraints for your task, however. If a solution didn't work in the past, it doesn't mean that it won't work this time. If experts say that an idea is bad, it certainly needs consideration. If this is how things always worked here, challenge it.

The best idea creators know: To generate a successful idea, you need to give the subconscious full freedom and generate many ideas, no matter how crazy, controversial or unrealistic. However, to be able to generate them you need to give your brain a direction: define an idea quota, deadline, resources and most importantly describe a task as specifically as possible. Your subconscious will generate amazing ideas for you, but before generating them it needs to know exactly what you want.

Essence of ideas

Lesson from the Market

Imagine that you live in a world where the success of each business is determined by an old and very wise man, whose name is Market. There is always a huge line of people, in front of his house, who want to hear his verdict about their business ideas. If Market says, "Your idea is excellent," then your product will be a big success; if Market says, "This idea isn't good," your product won't be in demand.

One day a young man came to Market and said, "I lived on an uninhabited island all my life and have never heard the ideas of others so you can be sure that my product is original. I spent 10 years on creating an original idea that can have a big impact on mankind and after many failures invented a wheel."

Market looked at the young man and smiled, "Young man, this idea isn't good. The wheel was invented thousands of years ago and people already use it in cars, bicycles, trains, buses and even airplanes."

Young man: "But, Market, I didn't know that the wheel was already invented. I created it completely independently. I can't believe that 10 years of my work are wasted."

Market said, "Young man, I see so many people who come to me with the hope of becoming successful but get disappointed just like you. Stay in my house as long as you want and observe which products I approve. If you are attentive enough, the next idea you bring will be a huge success."

Next in line was Steve Jobs. Market said, "Hi, Steve. What have you brought to me this time?"

"Market, I observed that when people unintentionally pull the power cord of the computer, it falls down and gets damaged. I want to solve this problem by creating a magnet that connects the computer to the power cord. When you abruptly pull the power cord the magnet will disconnect and the computer will be safe."

"Your idea is excellent, Steve." said Market.

The young man asked, "Market, I just talked with a woman from Japan and she said that in her country rice cookers with magnetic latches that prevent a spill have already been produced for many years. Steve's idea isn't original. Why did you approve it?"

"Young man, I don't care if an idea is fully original. People copy and build up on ideas of others every day. This is how progress in society is made. The only thing I care about is that your product is the best among those that are brought to me and that it can change the lives of people for the better. Steve's idea improves the experience of the laptop users and will be successful."

The young man carefully observed which ideas Market approved and by the end of the day asked, "Market, I see that among ideas that you approved were MTV, drive-thru banking and rollerblading. I learned that these ideas are a combination of the old ones. For example: MTV is a combination of music and television, drive-thru banking is a combination of a car and banking and rollerblading is a combination of ice skating and roller skating. These products aren't fully original, why did you let them be successful?"

"You see, young man, there is no such thing as an original idea. All ideas are either modifications or combinations of the old ones. The more old ideas you learn, the more material you have for creating your own ideas. I don't care how original your idea is, the only thing I care about is that your product makes the lives of other people better. Before you leave, please tell me what you learned today."

"Market, I learned that each idea is either a modification or combination of the old ones. I decided to learn as many ideas of others as I can to later adopt or combine them for creating my own successful products. However, the most important thing I learned is that successful ideas make people's lives better."

Market looked at the young man, winked and said, "I think that we will see each other often. I am looking forward to hearing your next idea."

Combine ideas

Make connections

When I studied at the University of Michigan, one day I asked my friend Martin, "Hey, Martin, how was your summer internship?" He said, "Andrii, I worked in a supply chain department of a large medical equipment producer. I have developed a new ordering strategy which saves the company over $10M per year. The company issued me a job offer and as a token of appreciation will pay for my education."

I asked, "Martin, how did you manage to get this idea?"

"Well, Andrii, actually I just brought directors of all the company divisions to the same room and asked how they place their orders now. We have taken the best ideas from all existing strategies and based on them, created a strategy that is a company-wide standard today."

Creativity researchers have discovered that all great ideas are combinations or modifications of the existing ones. Geniuses create their breakthrough inventions by making connections between existing ideas, just like Martin during his summer internship. Henry Ford once said, "The simple secret of my genius is that I created something new out of the ideas and inventions of others." Steve Jobs said, "When you ask creative people how they did something, they feel a little guilty because they didn't really do it; they just saw something. It seemed obvious to them after a while. That's because they were able to connect experiences they've had and synthesize new things." American advertising executive Jerry Della Femina said: "Creativity is about making a lot of quick connections — about the things you know, the things you've seen. The more you've done, the easier it is to make that jump."

Professor Dean Keith, in his research, found that creative geniuses generate more breakthrough ideas than other people. What he also found is that they generate many more useless and unsuccessful ideas. The creation of a breakthrough business idea depends on chance and geniuses increase its probability by making a lot of connections between random thoughts, experiences and ideas.

If you want to dramatically increase your effectiveness in producing great business ideas, make this your invocation:

"All ideas are a combination or modification of existing ideas. To increase the probability of creating a successful business idea, I will make more random combinations between thoughts, experiences and ideas every day."

Just focus your attention and think

When I studied at elementary school, our teacher once said, "Don't think about a yellow monkey." The entire class laughed because we all thought about the yellow monkey. In my imagination the monkey was sitting on a bench, then dancing and eventually sitting at the desk.

When you concentrate your attention on a particular object or a problem, after some time your brain will get bored and begin thinking about how to perceive it differently, decompose it into parts or connect with other thoughts, experiences or ideas. I am often asked, "Andrii, how should I be thinking?" and I answer, "Simply focus your attention on the problem and your creative mind will do the rest."

Leonardo da Vinci discovered that the human brain can't concentrate deliberately on two ideas no matter how different without forming connections between them, eventually.

Psychologists have discovered that our brain always tries to find patterns and sense in everything. If you concentrate on two absolutely dissimilar concepts, eventually the brain will build connections between them in order to make them a combination that makes sense. For example, if you think about a donkey and TV, your brain may generate the following ideas: a cartoon about a donkey, a TV in the form of a donkey, a donkey that carries TVs on its back, a TV producer logo in the form of donkey or a TV channel about donkeys.

When you want to generate a successful business idea, simply concentrate your attention on your problem and a random idea. The subconscious mind will deal with creating combinations and modifications. The more random ideas and thoughts your brain combines with your problem, the more chance you have of coming up with a really brilliant idea.

Exercise: Random objects

"Random objects" will develop your habit of combining seemingly unrelated objects to create new business ideas. The way you will generate ideas in this exercise is very similar to how business geniuses produce their best ideas.

Pick two random unrelated objects and make a connection between them in order to create a new product or a new business idea. Within 5 minutes generate as many combinations as possible and write them down. Don't try to make your ideas realistic, try to generate as many ideas as possible, no matter how crazy. You will always be able to think about how to make some of these ideas a reality and choose the most viable one later, however at this stage let your subconscious generate combinations without any limitations.

For example, if you pick soap and a car, the combinations may be: car in the form of a soap, use soap to wash a car, a car seat in the form of a soap, a bathroom in a car, soap used as a fuel instead of gasoline or a car that sprinkles soap on a street to wash it.

Do you see how this exercise can be applied in generating successful business ideas? Imagine that one object is a question you want to solve and a second object is a random item or idea. Do this exercise with many random items and ideas and eventually you will find a genius solution for your task. This is exactly the process that the world's best innovators use. Successful ideas are combinations of other ideas. And the most effective way to generate them is to make many combinations of random ideas. The more connections you make, the more likely you are to generate a successful idea.

When a chef wants to create a new, delicious dish he or she takes different ingredients from the refrigerator and combines or modifies them with a knife, a mixer or a cooker. The more a chef experiments, the higher are the chances to create a tasty original dish. In business, ingredients are ideas and life experiences that are stored in your memory. To create new combinations among the ideas (ingredients), instead of kitchen appliances, you use your subconscious mind. If you make it a habit to regularly focus attention on your task and random ideas, concepts and thoughts, your brain will generate a lot of ideas, some of which will make your business enormously successful.

Copy ideas

Before 1981 when Jack Welch became CEO of GE, the company was resistant to ideas or products "not invented here" and concentrated on creating all ideas within the organization's boundaries. Jack set a new vision, "Someone, somewhere has a better idea" and happily adapted these ideas for specific needs of the company. Within the next 20 years, GE's value rose 4,000% and Jack Welch was called CEO of the Century by Forbes magazine. In a documentary he said,

"It's a badge of honor to have found from Motorola a quality program, from HP a product development program, from Toyota an asset management system."

No matter how clever you are, no matter how purposeful you are, you will never be able to create more ideas than thousands of geniuses before you. If you want to become a successful business ideas creator, first you need to learn how to copy and then how to innovate on top of existing ideas. If you created an outstanding idea but later realized that it was created by someone in the past, you have wasted your time. Why? You could have copied and applied this idea to your business and spent time on creating new ideas on top of existing ideas. Your customers don't care who has created an idea, the only thing they care about is who has the best product and service on the market.

Do you know why ideas are not copyrightable? Because copying is how progress is made. All innovators copy ideas from each other and innovate on top of them. Imagine that the idea of producing a computer was owned by one company. If it were so, computers today would probably be extremely expensive and far less advanced.

The USA built its economy during the industrial revolution by copying ideas and technologies from Europe and later innovating on top of them. Japan built its prospering economy after World War II by imitating and copying U.S. and European technologies. Since the 1990s, China has been actively copying ideas and technologies from the USA, Europe and Japan and its economy is rapidly growing.

Innovations and business ideas depend on the exchange of ideas. New ideas are combinations or modifications of existing ideas. The more life experiences you have, the more ideas of others you know, the better ideas you will be able to build on top of them. With the development of the internet and cheap transportation, you have access to billions of ideas around the world. Learn them, copy them, modify them and you will be able to multiply many times your effectiveness at producing successful business ideas.

Very often people fall into the trap of thinking that the ideas they produce should be completely original, and significantly limit their creative productivity. Don't be one of them. If you realize that completely original ideas do not exist, stop trying to create something out of nothing and expose yourself as much as possible to ideas of others, you will increase your creative productivity many times.

Most everything I've done I've copied from somebody else. – Sam Walton

Good artists copy, great artists steal. – Pablo Picasso

We have always been shameless about stealing great ideas. – Steve Jobs

When people call something "original," nine out of ten times they just don't know the references or the original sources involved. What a good artist understands is that nothing comes from nowhere. All creative work builds on what came before. Nothing is completely original. – Jonathan Lethem

Don't strive to create the most original ideas, strive to create the best products and services on the market. Learn and copy great ideas as much as possible. It is essential for creating excellent ideas and your success in business.

Adopt ideas

My friend Dmitriy from the Ukraine told a story about how his mother became successful in business. In the 1990s, Dmitriy's mother Irina had a dream to open a pharmacy and mortgaged her apartment to purchase a stock of pharmaceuticals. Irina was selling them in a kiosk until she saved enough money to open a pharmacy. Irina went to Germany for 2 weeks and visited hundreds of pharmacies around the country. She observed how pharmacies operate in Germany and wrote down all the interesting ideas she noticed.

After coming home, Irina adopted these ideas to the Ukrainian market and implemented them in her own pharmacy. After a few months it became the best and most popular pharmacy in the town. Now she owns over 20 pharmacies, lives in a huge house and is a multimillionaire.

Thomas Edison, one of the greatest inventors of the 20th century, believed that seeing analogies is key to creating successful ideas. He said, "Make it a habit to keep on the lookout for novel and interesting ideas that others have used successfully. Your idea needs to be original only in its adaptation to the problem you are working on."

One of the most popular TV shows in the Ukraine is *Ukraine's Got Talent*. In this show, amateur or unknown performers show their talents on stage. They are judged by 3 celebrities and the audience votes. The final show of the first season was watched by 18.6 million people, which is more than 40% of Ukraine's population. Do Ukrainians care that the format of the show was copied and adopted from

America's Got Talent and *Britain's Got Talent*? No, the only thing they care is that it is very interesting to watch.

Constantly think about how good ideas can be adopted from other countries, other businesses or products. Irina's story isn't unique; enormous fortunes have been made by adopting existing ideas.

Early adopters win

In 2004, Mark Zuckerberg, then a student at Harvard University, developed and launched Facebook social network. Facebook became a multibillion-dollar company and the most popular social network in the world with over 750 million active users in 2010.

In 2006, having just graduated from St. Petersburg State University, Pavel Durov adopted the idea of Facebook for Russian-speaking countries and launched Vkontakte social network. In 2012 Vkontakte became the 19th most visited website in the world and the 2nd most popular social network in Europe.

Technically, a social network isn't difficult to develop. In fact, today you can create your own social network in a matter of minutes even if you don't know how to code. Many thousands of people worldwide copied the idea of Facebook and launched their own social networks, very few of which became popular. You might ask, "What is the difference between Pavel Durov and thousands of other people who launched their social networks but failed to make them successful?"

Pavel Durov was one of the first users of Facebook. He noticed the potential of the social network idea far before

Facebook became known by millions of people around the world. In 2008, many of my friends in the Ukraine became users of Facebook and Vkontakte almost simultaneously. Today they get invited to some newly created social networks almost every month but don't join them. Why? Firstly, because they want to be members of the biggest social networks and secondly because they can't actively participate in more than 2-3 social networks.

Constantly look for emerging business ideas; once they turn into billion-dollar businesses it might be too late to develop a successful business by adopting them. You will have the biggest benefit of copying them if you notice their potential earlier than the rest of the world. Become an early adopter of new services and products at the stage when they are only on the way to being widely used. The earlier you see a potential in a particular idea, the more value you will get from adopting it in your own business.

The same ideas may come to the minds of many people, however if you get the idea earlier than others, implement it earlier and promote it earlier, you will have a significant advantage. Timing is very critical for the success of your ideas. Spot opportunities early because early adopters win.

Think differently

On the opening day of *The Hunger Games* movie, my wife and I were looking for a parking spot in front of the cinema in Santa Clara, CA. It was dark, it was raining and the parking lot was fully packed with cars. There was obviously not a single spot available, however we hoped that somebody would be leaving the parking lot and we could take the space.

In 15 minutes Olena said, "There are dozens of cars besides us circling the parking lot and even if some space frees up, it will be taken in a heartbeat." I thought, "We should either go home or think differently from everybody else. What place would nobody consider for parking?"

In a few minutes, an idea came to my head, we drove away from the main entrance, turned and found that almost all the parking spots at the back of the cinema were free. I parked the car. Within 2 minutes, we walked to the main entrance and enjoyed the excellent movie.

The market is like a big parking lot. If you are doing what everybody else is doing, it will be very difficult to compete and build a profitable business. When you think about the problem, consider what ideas you created, what competitors are doing and then change the direction of your thinking. To create successful ideas and find profitable business niches, challenge the status quo, look at the problem from different angles and make it your mantra: "Think differently."

Raw materials for ideas

Why you need raw materials

When I was 15, my family moved and during my last year before college I went to a high school which was not only closer to my house, but also significantly stronger in math.

I approached my new math teacher, Alexander, and said, "Alexander, I want to achieve the maximum I can in competitive math and I am willing to work as hard as possible this year. I know that you prepared several international level math Olympiad winners. Please suggest what I can work on at home in addition to regular classes."

He said, "You see, Andrii, to win a math Olympiad, relying only on agility of the brain isn't enough. You should also rely on your competitive math experience.

"I will give you books with collections of problems from past national and international math competitions. Think about each problem yourself for some time, and then read the solution in the back of the book. After a while, you will notice patterns and memorize various approaches for tackling problems. The more solutions of others you read, the more approaches for solving problems are in your arsenal and the more likely you are to solve a math problem.

"Once you face a problem in a math competition, you will have many different approaches in your arsenal to begin solving it and coupled with agility of the brain you will become a very strong contestant who can win."

A new idea is a modification or combination of old ones. Old ideas are a raw material for creative thinking. The more ideas of other people you know, the more connections your brain will be able to make and the more likely you are to create an interesting and valuable business idea.

Expose yourself to new experiences

One day little Jimmy went to his best friend Suzy's house and noticed what beautiful constructions she built from a Lego set. He looked at cars, ships and castles and decided, "I want to build beautiful Lego constructions, too."

Jimmy took two little pieces of a Lego set that he owned. He spent hours looking at them and trying to put them together in all possible combinations but realized that no matter what he did these 2 pieces never looked like a car, a ship or a castle. He went to Suzy and said, "Suzy, I am just not creative enough to build beautiful Lego constructions." Suzy looked at him, smiled and said, "Jimmy, you are more than talented for creating beautiful Lego constructions. You just don't have enough constructor pieces. I have been collecting my Lego pieces for years and now have thousands of them. If you had as many pieces as I do, you would easily create even better constructions."

Ideas are combinations of other ideas and the more diverse life experiences you have, the more different ideas you will be able to construct. Many people say, "I can't create great business ideas. I am not creative." However, the true reason why they fail is that they have too few different experiences in their memory to construct new ideas from.

The world's greatest thinkers have an insatiable curiosity and actively seek new experiences that can increase the amount of their creative constructor pieces. They travel, make new acquaintances, try various hobbies, attend conferences and seminars, and read books, magazines and blogs.

People whose life follows the same pattern for years may find themselves in a situation like little Jimmy who tried to create something incredible from just several pieces of a Lego set. Constantly bombard your brain with new ideas and experiences which will become raw materials for your future successful business ideas. The more different experiences you have had in life, the more ideas of others you have learned, the more creative combinations your brain will be able to make and the more valuable ideas it will generate. If you want to be a world-class thinker, a quest for new creative raw materials should become your habit.

Creativity is just connecting things. When you ask creative people how they did something, they feel a little guilty because they didn't really do it, they just saw something. It seemed obvious to them after a while. That's because they were able to connect experiences they've had and synthesize new things. And the reason they were able to do that was that they've had more experiences or they have thought more about their experiences than other people. Unfortunately, that's too rare a commodity. A lot of people in our industry haven't had very diverse experiences. So they don't have enough dots to connect, and they end up with very linear solutions without a broad perspective on the problem. – Steve Jobs

Write ideas down

When I studied at school, my math teacher kept repeating, "If you haven't written down a solution for the problem, you haven't solved a problem." Before I took this advice seriously, quite often I had to say, "I solved this problem yesterday, but just forgot the solution."

If there was just one tip I could give, that would help you the most in creating successful business ideas, it would be this: "Always write down your ideas! Write each idea down as soon as it comes to your head or they will go as quickly as they came. Write down the idea no matter when and where it came." Capturing ideas has several benefits:

Firstly, the ideas are saved and can be used later. For any successful business ideas creator, not writing down an idea looks even more ridiculous than burning $100 bills with a lighter. Ideas are treasures and should always be saved.

Secondly, writing down an idea sends a signal to your subconscious mind, "Thank you very much for generating this wonderful idea. I highly appreciate what you do for me. Please generate more ideas." If the subconscious mind feels appreciated, it will work harder and generate even more wonderful ideas for you. Imagine that you say something to your friend, and he or she doesn't listen. You repeat a second time but he or she doesn't care about what you say again. Eventually you stop talking. The same happens with your right brain if you don't appreciate ideas that it generates.

Finally, when you have many ideas on paper you can easily switch between them. Each idea can be modified or combined with other ideas to create new ideas. For example when Edison's Ore Milling Company proved to be financially unprofitable, he looked through his notebooks with ideas. Edison figured out that his company had a very similar business model to one in the cement industry and formed Edison Portland Cement in 1899.

Thomas Edison, Benjamin Franklin, Leonardo da Vinci, the Wright brothers, Virginia Woolf, Carl Jung, Charles Darwin and thousands of other famous entrepreneurs, innovators, writers, scientists and artists carried notebooks and wrote down all their ideas. This habit played an important role in their success.

What to do if the idea caught you off guard?

Imagine that just before you fall asleep an amazing idea comes to your head. You might think, "I am too tired to write down the idea. I will do it first thing in the morning." Guess what, once you wake up the idea will be gone and may never come to you again.

The best ideas often come when you least expect them: in a grocery store, while you exercise in the gym or sleep. Although, writing down an idea often may seem terribly inconvenient, always write it down no matter when and where it came. If you got an idea at 3 in the morning, wake up and write it down. If you got an idea during an important business meeting, take a pen and write it down. If you got an idea in a grocery store, find a way to write it down. This habit will have an enormous impact on your success in business and life.

You might ask, "Andrii, what if there is no way for me to write down an idea? For example, I am driving a car or presenting in front of a large audience. Can I remember the idea to write it down later?"

One day I went jogging to the stadium and was thinking about what makes a book memorable and interesting to read. Three valuable ideas popped up in my head: "The text should be succinct. The book should have stories or at least metaphors. Knowing what to leave out is even more important than what to include in the book." I thought, "Hey, I have to either stop jogging and go home or remember the ideas for the next 45 minutes and write them down later."

Memory experts have discovered that people don't remember ideas or facts, they only remember pictures. So, if you want to remember an idea, you have to associate it with a picture in your imagination. I associated "succinct" with a "tennis ball," "leaving information out" with "throwing away trash" and "telling metaphors" with a wise man sitting in a lotus pose. I then combined 3 pictures into one: a wise man throwing away trash with his right hand and holding a tennis ball in his left hand. Using this technique I was able not only to recall and write down these 3 ideas in 45 minutes, but also to remember them even years after the day they came to me.

Businesses become enormously successful or go bankrupt because of great ideas or lack of them. Make it a habit to write down ideas as soon as they come into your head no matter what. Even if you are walking in a desert or running a marathon and there is no way to write down an idea immediately, associate it with a picture in your imagination to not let it go. Great idea creators say that writing down all their ideas was essential for the breakthroughs in business, science or art that they made. This habit will increase your productivity in creating high-quality business ideas multiple times and have an enormous impact on your success in life.

Beliefs of the world-class innovator

Belief and desire

Your subconscious mind is an incredibly powerful thinking mechanism that is programmed by your desires. The more you want to solve a particular task, the harder your subconscious will think to find a solution.

For example, if you say, "It would be nice to find a solution for my task" your subconscious would do nothing. If you say, "I really want to find a solution" your subconscious would think and give you some ideas. However, if you say, "I am obsessed with what I am doing and have a burning desire to find a solution" your subconscious will think at full capacity and generate a lot of high-quality ideas that will make your business successful.

The best business innovators know the secret of effective thinking and if you ask any of them about his or her success secret, the answer is always the same: "Do what you are passionate about." This advice is very simple and you may have heard it numerous times. Your success in generating ideas will depend on whether you act upon it or not.

Even if you have a burning desire to generate ideas you may block your subconscious by thinking, "I am not sure if I can generate good ideas," "I can't generate good ideas" or "I will see if I can generate good ideas or not." The most important belief of the great thinkers is "I will definitely find an excellent solution for my task." Your subconscious is very sensitive to your beliefs. If you doubt that you will generate great ideas, the subconscious will be blocked by your analytical brain. If you are 100% confident that you will generate great ideas, it will be unstoppable and excellent ideas will flow into your brain as quickly as possible.

When I asked my friend Max, who's been working over 10 years as a creative director in a world-famous company, what is most important for generating high-quality ideas he said, "Andrii, it is your 100% belief that you will generate them."

Remember the magic induction, "I have a burning desire to create successful business ideas and a 100% confidence that I will generate them." It turns ordinary people into the world's greatest thinkers.

Nothing great was ever accomplished without enthusiasm. – Ralph Waldo Emerson

It's very hard to succeed in something unless you take the first step – which is to become very interested in it. – Sir William Osler

Visualization

When I was 22, I had a burning desire to receive a Masters of Business Administration degree from one of the top 10 business schools in the USA. I realized, "The average candidate is 28 years old and has at least 5 years of experience in finance, supply chain management, marketing or strategy, which I don't. Basically my chances of getting accepted are slim."

I drew on an A4 sheet of paper a picture of where I was a student at one of the top 10 MBA schools and hung it on the wall near my desk. Every time I looked at it, I imagined that I had already been accepted and enjoyed my time in the MBA program. Within the next several months, I had generated numerous amazing ideas of how to increase my chances of getting accepted. And the miracle happened. I became the youngest student at the MBA program at Michigan Ross School of Business and even received a generous scholarship. Later, I learned that the reason I was accepted to one of the top 10 business schools was the law of attraction that successful idea generators have used for thousands of years. The law of attraction says, "You get what you think about, because your subconscious draws actions, thoughts and events to your life based on the program you set." Let's see how it works.

Every time you imagine that you already achieved a goal, your subconscious receives a task, "Please make my dream a reality." When you visualize your desire often, your creative brain thinks about potential ideas and solutions actively. Eventually you get necessary answers and make your dream a reality.

Draw a picture of your goal and hang it near your desk or bed. Every time you look at it imagine as vividly as possible that you have already achieved your dream. Your subconscious will get activated and will think about ways to make the picture from your imagination a reality. You can be sure that one day your goal will be achieved, no matter how big it is.

The law of attraction is one of the most effective techniques that exist not only for generating ideas but also for achieving goals. Use it for small goals that are achievable within a week, use it for average goals that are achievable within a month, and use it for huge strategic goals that you want to achieve within a decade. You can use the law of attraction as many times as you want and every time it will bring you whatever you ask for.

Visualization works perfectly in combination with the "Think and Rest" technique. Remember also that to make your subconscious think actively you need to have a burning desire to find a solution and a 100% confidence that you will generate great ideas.

Relocate to a high-performance state

One day, while a student at the University of Michigan, I went to a bar with my friends and several alumni to celebrate the end of the school year. After we ordered drinks and started a conversation, I said something funny and everybody laughed. I told another joke and everybody laughed, again. That afternoon the best comedians would have envied my ability to tell jokes on the spot, and for about 2 hours everyone was laughing really hard. I often struggle to come up with a great joke, but that afternoon I couldn't stop the flow of amazing jokes coming to my mind.

Do you remember a time when you were much more effective at generating ideas than usual? Researchers who model and replicate behavior of successful people found that the state we are in has a huge effect on our ability to generate ideas and we are most effective in a high-performance state.

In a high-performance state, people are relaxed, excited, lively, open and confident. The opposite is also true. If you become relaxed, excited, lively, open and confident simultaneously, you will get into the high-performance state and become dramatically more effective at producing ideas.

When actors play a role and want to convey a particular emotion of the character, they need to evoke it in themselves. They remember a situation from life when they felt this emotion clearly, relive it in their imagination and very soon begin to feel the emotion. This technique from the world of acting will help you with getting into a high-performance state.

To get into a high-performance state, you need to become simultaneously relaxed, excited, lively, open and confident. When these 5 states are combined, their individual effects on performance increase many times.

Relaxed

The more you relax, the more access you get to your creative brain and the more likely you are to generate successful business ideas. That's why we often come to original ideas while sleeping, taking a warm shower or meditating. A relaxed state is essential for activating the subconscious mind and being creative.

Relax all the muscles in your body completely except for the ones you need to stay upright. First, flex all your muscles and then quickly relax them. Relax all the muscles from your head to your feet. Pay attention to your breathing. Notice that each time you breathe and exhale, your body relaxes more and more until you are fully relaxed.

Excited

Imagine how awesome it will be when you have generated an excellent business idea. Imagine how your life will change, what you will be doing and what your relatives and friends will be telling you. Relieve your wonderful future in imagination and increase excitement until you feel as excited as a 5-year-old kid before getting a Christmas present.

Lively

Become energetic. Feel the power within you and your readiness to do something. To become energetic, jump, dance, do physical exercise or just remember how it felt when you did something active. If you imagine it clearly enough, your nervous system won't notice any difference. Remember, however, that you need to build up your energy while staying completely relaxed. As soon as you notice tension – relax yourself. It might seem impossible to be lively and relaxed simultaneously, but it is easy. It's an amazing feeling of outside calmness and internal readiness.

Open

Zen Buddhism has a concept of "beginner's mind." Zen teachers say that having a beginner's mind means facing life like a child, being full of curiosity, amazement and open to anything new. Openness is one of the foundations of creativity. Be open to all opportunities and ideas, no matter how crazy they look at first glance.

Remember a time when you were ready to accept anything that the world has to offer. You don't know what will happen in the next moment, but it is not important because you are ready to accept anything. Build up a feeling of openness until you can clearly feel it.

Confident

If you think that you are not creative or if you doubt that you can come up with an amazing idea, your subconscious will be blocked and will indeed not generate successful ideas. Being 100% confident that great ideas will come to you is one of the most important things in the idea generation process.

Recall a situation from your life when you felt absolutely confident in yourself. Maybe you said or did something you were 100% sure about. Relive it as clearly as you can and feel what you felt at that time. While building up a feeling of confidence, remain open, lively, excited and relaxed.

Again

Repeat again everything mentioned above! Every time you increase the intensity of each feeling, make sure you stay simultaneously relaxed, excited, lively, open and confident. Go through this list several times and very soon you will get into a high-productivity state.

A high-performance state is a state in which the creative brain works most effectively. I highly recommend getting into a high-performance state whenever you need to generate ideas. This state will do magic with your ability to create successful business ideas.

Generating ideas is a game

When I was about 12 years old, I had a huge fear. I was afraid of getting beaten up by bullies on the street. I was so scared to go to school every day that my parents put me into the Kiokushin Karate school to get this fear out of me.

Every training session, after stretching and practicing punches, we had practice fights. I was fighting against older, bigger and more experienced guys. It was painful, unpleasant and that time lasted an eternity for me.

One day our trainer, Alexander, said, "Everyone, please sit in a circle. I have to tell you something." What he said not only changed my attitude towards karate and fighting but also my attitude towards generating ideas.

"Guys, don't fear the pain from the punches. Have an attitude towards a fight as you would towards a game. Here you missed a punch, here you managed to hit your opponent and there you made a successful block. It's fun! It's interesting, exciting and challenging!" These words struck a chord with me and I will remember them forever.

Once I started to think about the fight as a game, I forgot about the pain but instead enjoyed the challenge. My parents found it difficult to believe, but after 2 months I even volunteered to participate in the Kyiv city karate championship.

The fight lasted a minute and a half. I punched, kicked and made blocks, but most often I was punched. After 45 seconds, I felt completely exhausted, like I couldn't even raise my hands, much less punch. The audience raved, "Andrii! Andrii! Kick his ass! Kill him!" When you hear your name cheered, it should give you more strength and power to win, but in my case it was the opposite. Guess what? My opponent's name was also Andrii! He had a green belt and more than 7 years of experience in karate.

I lost that fight. I was beaten up. But it was truly fun! Few things can compare to it.

After the fight, the trainer called me and said, "Andrii, you fought like a lion. I am proud of you. And by the way, you really challenged greatly this guy who won two previous city championships." Those were the nicest words that I ever heard. The next year I won many fights and even received a karate blue belt.

When you fight, winning or losing depends a lot on your attitude. If you are serious and think about how bad it will be if you lose, your subconscious will be blocked and won't give you great ideas about how to punch or block punches. Fighters who win are passionate about martial arts, have fun and consider a fight as a game.

According to researchers, over 98% of children younger than 10 years of age possess genius-level creativity. Children generate a lot of original ideas and they always have fun while generating them. When you have fun, you forget about time, you forget about mealtimes and activate your subconscious. It processes millions of thoughts at full capacity and eventually gives you amazing ideas in the form of a gut feeling, a hunch or intuition. There is a guaranteed way to not generate good ideas. Being serious! Unfortunately, seriousness is the state in which the majority of adults remain most of the time.

An environment of playfulness and humor is highly conducive to creativity. While you have fun, and your attitude towards the ideas generation process is as to a game, you are relaxed, excited, lively, open and confident. These are the characteristics of the high-performance state in which ideas are generated most effectively. Increase the amount of time you have fun in your life, do what you are passionate about and the amount of successful ideas that you generate will skyrocket. Whenever you are thinking hard about ideas and they are not coming, tell yourself, "Don't be so serious! Have fun! Generating ideas is an interesting and exciting game!"

Serious people have few ideas. People with ideas are never serious. — Paul Valery

Idea refinement

Idea evolution

Imagine that you were an inventor in the 14th century, went to the palace of the king and said, "Hurray, I invented a computer. Your Majesty, my new invention will allow you to browse the internet, read books, check emails and even watch movies." The king might say, "Are you nuts? We don't have electricity yet. Even though you are really smart, this invention is useless."

Motorola created the first handheld mobile phone. Apple created a mobile phone with a touch screen and millions of supported applications. Skype created an application that allows free video conversations through the internet. Motorola, Apple, Skype and thousands of other companies made enormous amounts of money just on the idea of the phone. Each idea evolves with time and to build a profitable business you need to make not more than one step in the evolution.

Don't try to create something unseen before and jump over many steps of evolution right away. Do sequential improvements. If you invented an electronic book reader device in the 14th century, your invention would be useless and ahead of its time. However, if you invented a printing press like Gutenberg, you would make a mark in history and make the world a better place.

Don't strive to be perfect, strive for continuous improvement

The biggest blocks to creativity are striving for perfection and fear of risk. Failures and imperfection are essential components of the successful idea generation process.

The initial ideas that you create often have flaws and require refinement before they are implemented. If you strive to create a perfect idea that will succeed guaranteed, you block your creativity and will only be able to reiterate old ideas that worked in the past.

When great writers write a book, they first write everything that comes to their mind on paper. Then this initial draft goes through many iterations of editing and becomes a great book. When you think about a question, your subconscious will rarely give you a fully refined answer; most often it is just a hint, an insight or a partial idea. Just like a writer edits his or her writing, you should improve your ideas before they become products, processes or actions. Don't strive to create perfect ideas, strive to create many ideas. They can always be improved later.

Modifying an existing product or service

The Transformer and SCAMPER techniques are proven to be invaluable for creating successful business ideas. These two techniques can help you generate a lot of great ideas necessary to create a profitable business, effective process or popular product.

Transformer

A Transformer technique is very simple but will allow you to create very successful businesses by challenging the status quo.

List rules and parameters of the business and then challenge them. Changing the rules may create an idea for a new successful business or a way to transform an existing one. Let's review how the Transformer technique can be applied in 3 examples below.

In a zoo animals live in cages and a zoo is open during the daytime. Let's challenge these rules. "Animals move freely around the zoo and it is open during nighttime." The Singapore zoo implemented this idea in a very popular attraction called Night Safari. Visitors travel in a tram across 7 geographical zones and observe nocturnal animals in their natural habitat. http://www.nightsafari.com.sg

A traditional circus features separate performances of acrobats, animals and clowns without a common theme. Guy Laliberte challenged this assumption and said, "I will create a circus show with a common theme and with only acrobats." He created Cirque du Soleil which is a billion-dollar business and is extremely popular around the world. http://www.cirquedusoleil.com

Bands play music on real instruments such as a guitar, a piano or a violin. The band plays music and the audience listens. Recycled Percussion band challenged these assumptions. In addition to traditional instruments, the group uses buckets and recycled materials. Each audience member receives an instrument with a drumstick and actively participates in the performance. After watching Recycled Percussion in Las Vegas, my dad said it was the best show he has ever seen. http://www.recycledpercussionband.com

Just because things have always been done in a certain way in business doesn't mean they can't be done better or differently. Get in a habit of listing characteristics of a business or a process and thinking about how to challenge them. Using the Transformer technique, you will be able to transform your existing business or find an idea for a new successful business. The best idea creators constantly challenge status quo, assumptions, rules and beliefs. Always ask, "How can I break this rule? What if I challenge this belief?"

SCAMPER

Remember what ideas are created from? Ideas are modifications or combinations of other ideas. SCAMPER (Substitute, Combine, Adapt, Magnify or Minimize, Put to other use, Eliminate, Rearrange or Reverse) is a very popular creative technique, because of its effectiveness for generating high-quality business ideas. SCAMPER allows you to apply most common modifications to the product or process and create new business ideas. Imagine that you parked your car near a café. You entered into the building, the waiter brought a menu and you ordered a dinner. After the meal you asked for a bill and left a tip. Let's use the SCAMPER technique for this regular café to see which new business ideas we can generate.

Substitute. Let's substitute driving to the café to the café coming to your house. Do you see which business ideas we can create based on this substitution? Pizza delivery services use this exact business model. You call the phone number, order your meal and it is delivered to your house in less than an hour.

Combine. Let's combine a café and a thrill ride. For example, a result can be a Belgian Dinner in The Sky restaurant service which uses a crane to lift people, dinners and tables 150 feet into the air. Forbes magazine called it one of the world's ten most unusual restaurants.

Adapt. Let's adapt a café for kids. How might such a café look? All dishes have funny titles adapted for kids and are served with a toy. The café has a playground and waiters are dressed in costumes of characters from popular cartoons. When I was in New York for the first time, a tour guide showed a doll store. This store has a café where girls can drink tea with their dolls.

Magnify or minimize. Let's reduce the number of items on the menu to several drinks and sandwiches. As a result we may get a fast food restaurant such as McDonald's, Burger King or KFC.

Now let's reduce the number of dishes to just three. As a result we can get a business lunch combo that the café offers from noon until 3 p.m.

Put to other use. The building of the café can be used to create a hairdressing salon, a pharmacy or a shop. Dining tables can be used as office desks. The kitchen can produce cooked food that will be sold through supermarkets or sandwiches that will be sold through gas stations.

Eliminate. Let's eliminate a building of the café. As a result we may have a drive-in café where you order and eat food while sitting in a car. Let's eliminate the waiters and we can get a help-yourself café where you put food on your plate yourself and later pay for it at the counter.

Rearrange or reverse. Let's reverse a statement, "Visitors should leave tips for waiters" to "Visitors shouldn't leave tips." As a result we can have a café where waiters don't receive tips.

To be honest I hate paying tips. When I lived in Ann Arbor, Michigan, one day, while walking along the street, I stumbled upon a café with a sign on the door: "We don't take tips." I entered and placed an order. When the waitress arrived she said, "Here is your meal. And I just want to remind you that our café has a no tips policy." Should I tell you that I became a regular visitor?

SCAMPER and Transformer are thinking techniques that can bring you a lot of successful business ideas. Apply them occasionally to see if you can improve your existing business or start a new one. These techniques will help your subconscious see new opportunities quicker. Some of these opportunities will eventually turn into successful businesses.

 Creativity in business is all about asking questions and thinking about answers. SCAMPER and Transformer help you to ask some of the good questions; your subconscious will generate ideas for you.

Mistakes lead to progress

Creativity is a probability game

One day there lived a young man called James who decided to open his own business. James thought, "I have an idea for a product that will change the world!" For 2 months James worked on developing his product and setting up the marketing campaign. Every morning he woke up with excitement, began working and finished only very late at night. This was the happiest time in James's life because he did what he loved and what he believed in. When the product was finally launched, James didn't sell anything and realized that nobody in the market wanted it. He thought, "I just don't have entrepreneurial talent! What did I hope for? I am not the business shark, just an ordinary James."

People tend to take it very personally when their ideas fail. The story about James is a story about millions of entrepreneurs worldwide. Some of them become very sad after the first couple of failures and stop trying new ideas, others realize that failures are an essential part of success and succeed.

Nature creates multiple species and lets a process of natural selection decide which will survive. Ninety-five percent of new species die and only the few strongest survive. Great idea creators know that just like in nature, to create a successful business you need to implement multiple ideas and let the market decide which of them will survive.

Research shows that successful artists, composers, scientists, writers and entrepreneurs not only succeed more often than others but also fail significantly more. They know that creativity is a probability game and the more ideas you implement, the more successful ones will be among them.

If you want to become good at business, make sure that your attitude towards failures is as follows: "Creativity is a probability game. I am excited to fail because the more I fail the more successful I become."

Failures are a valuable experience

One of the greatest scientists of the 20th century, Thomas Edison, created 10,000 prototypes before presenting to the world a commercially viable light bulb. He said, "I have not failed 10,000 times. I have not failed once. I have succeeded in proving that those 10,000 ways will not work. When I have eliminated the ways that will not work, I will find the way that will work."

The greatest innovators know that to become successful you need to make good decisions. Good decisions come from experience and experience comes from bad decisions. When you fail, you learn what doesn't work and why. This experience is the reason why you eventually succeed.

Everybody knows the Apple computer that Steve Jobs created, the light bulb that Edison invented and the theory of relativity that Einstein developed. Few people know that these great thinkers also implemented a large amount of ideas that didn't succeed. In creative thinking, quality comes from quantity and the more successful businesses you create the more failures you encounter along the way.

The best innovators fail often. The best innovators fail eagerly. The best innovators know that they are successful because they have failed more than others. The more ideas you generate and the more of them you implement, the sooner you will create something great. If you want to become a world-class ideas creator, expect that many of your ideas will fail, some will succeed and a few will have potential to change the world.

Become an accidental entrepreneur

One day in 1928 a Scottish biologist, Alexander Fleming, forgot to clean his laboratory before going on vacation. In 2 weeks, when Alexander returned from vacation, he saw that one of the staphylococcus culture plates in the corner of the laboratory was contaminated by a strange fungus, which prevented the growth of staphylococcus bacteria. After examination of the fungus, he noticed that it produced a substance that killed many disease-causing bacteria. This observation led Alexander to develop penicillin, an antibiotic that made one of the biggest breakthroughs in medicine and allowed the treatment of such dangerous illnesses as meningitis, gonorrhea and syphilis.

Penicillin, pacemakers, plastic, vulcanized rubber, Teflon, corn flakes, saccharin and numerous other inventions were made by accident. In business, successful ideas are often created by chance after a mistake, failure or coincidence, and your goal is to increase the probability of this chance many times.

Talk to as many people as you can, travel, experiment in business, read books, do different hobbies and try everything you haven't tried before. Coming up with a successful business idea by accident is the same as winning a lottery. Every life experience you have gives you an additional lottery ticket. The more active and versatile your life is, the higher are your chances to win a creative lottery and stumble upon a successful business idea.

Many people lose opportunities that life gives them, because they blindly follow their preconceived plan. Creative geniuses look forward to accidental discoveries and once they notice something interesting, drop everything they do to study it.

Appreciate all ideas that come to your head even if they are irrelevant to what you work on. Look forward to accidental discoveries and once you win the creative lottery, do everything to save, analyze and implement the successful business idea that came to your head. Be sure that some of these accidental ideas will have the same impact on your business as penicillin had on medicine.

Physical Fitness, Sleep and Energy

Good sleep and physical exercises not only help to maintain good health but also stimulate generation of business ideas.

Sleep

Many people think, "To become successful I need to do more work and stay awake longer. Time spent sleeping is time wasted." In fact, most productive thinkers sleep on average longer than other people.

The subconscious mind is responsible for generating successful business ideas and it works best when your conscious mind is inactive and especially well during sleep. If you need a good idea you are much more likely to generate it after 8 hours of healthy sleep than after a night of staring at the computer screen.

The best inventors are aware of the power of sleep and use it daily. In fact, they create a lot of breakthrough ideas during sleep or a nap. In terms of generating successful business ideas, sleep is certainly not a waste of time. In fact, it can be the most productive time of the day.

Physical exercises

Researchers found that regular physical exercises improve memory, mood and creative thinking. If you need to create good ideas or prepare for an exam, you will be more productive after jogging, swimming or taking a dancing class.

Physical exercises stimulate greatly the creative brain to think during the ideas incubation period. When you dance, run or swim, the conscious brain rests and the subconscious mind processes millions of thoughts. You might realize that the problem you have been thinking about the whole day is often solved either while you exercise or soon after.

The world's best thinkers know that if you need good ideas regularly, exercises are not optional because without them after a couple of weeks or months the creative productivity drops. Exercise at least two or three times per week and it will not only boost your energy but will also make you a better thinker.

You can't create anything awesome if you are not well rested or if you have low energy. Sleep well and exercise regularly. These two habits will not only keep you healthy but will also allow you to create a lot of excellent business ideas.

If you are stuck with a problem, go to sleep or exercise. Very likely the insight will come to you during the next thinking session.

Ideas-stimulating environment

Where to think best

Change the surroundings

One day, I was waiting for my wife on the bench in the hairdressing salon. I opened a notebook and began writing. The place was noisy and the bench uncomfortable but somehow my brain turned into an exceptionally creative mode and I wrote perhaps my best story ever.

For your brain it doesn't matter where to think; in a comfortable corner office, in a hairdressing salon or in a supermarket line. What is really important is that places where you think are occasionally changed. Our brain is stimulated by images that it sees. If you work in the same place every day and see the same images, eventually your creative brain will become lazy.

Your brain can be extremely productive in a hotel, in an airport lounge, in the back seat of a cab, in an office, at home, in a café or any other place, but under one condition. Locations where you think are occasionally changed. If your eyes see different surroundings during thinking sessions, your subconscious will be stimulated and will think at full capacity.

For an idea generation session, extract yourself from your everyday surroundings and go to a café, a library or a park. Thinking about ideas for 2 hours at an unusual location may bring you more ideas than a day of staring at the computer screen in the office. Don't think too hard about where to think, because any place that you don't visit regularly will stimulate your creative brain. If you asked me, "Andrii, where do you get your best ideas?" I would say, "In a hotel room, while taking a walk, in the shower, in a supermarket, during a boring meeting, when I jog at a stadium, in a cab, in the airport or while chatting with a friend in a café." The only thing that is common among places where our brains generate their best ideas is that they are different from where we spend most of our working time.

NeuroLeadership Institute's executive director, David Rock, surveyed over 6,000 people to discover where their best ideas were generated. Only 10% of respondents indicated that their best ideas came to them in the office, 39% said that their best ideas came to them at home and 51% said that their best ideas came to them neither at home nor at the office, but while traveling, jogging, eating in a café, at the park, in the swimming pool, at the beach, in a museum etc. This research confirms that the best ideas are generated when we get out of the surroundings that the brain sees the majority of the time.

In the office or at home

You can change scenery even without leaving an office. Simply changing pictures on the walls or moving from one desk to another may improve your creative thinking. Many companies that rely on creativity have many locations inside the office building where each employee can work.

When you work at home, occasionally change locations. Work in a bedroom, in a living room or in a kitchen. Sit on a sofa, at a desk or in an armchair. Changing locations inside your house can improve productivity of your thinking.

As a creative thinker, you should get used to changing scenery more often than other people. Travel whenever you can, work outside of your home or office whenever you can, utilize places where people kill time as your creative studio whenever you can. The more you change locations where you think, the more actively your brain will think and the more successful business ideas you will be able to produce. Change the rooms and locations in the rooms where you think to not let your brain become stale.

Go for a walk

Jean-Jacques Rousseau, the famous French philosopher, Johann Wolfgang von Goethe and Sigmund Freud created some of their best ideas while taking a walk. Taking a walk put them into creative mode and accelerated their thinking.

Walking is a monotonous physical activity that stimulates your subconscious mind and increases your chances to come up with a really good idea. When the landscape constantly changes in front of your eyes, the creative brain gets nurtured by fresh images and thinks more productively. If you are ever stuck and can't come up with good ideas, simply go for a walk. Great thinkers have been using a walk for centuries as a magic pill for stimulating their subconscious mind and getting into the creative state.

Any place is good

Think about ideas at places where most other people are just killing time: while walking to a parking lot, while waiting for a bus, while sitting at a boring meeting, at the airport or in the supermarket line. This habit will significantly improve the quality and quantity of ideas that you produce.

Some people think, "Creativity is a difficult and unpleasant job because I have to sit for hours and stare at the wall until a good idea comes." In fact, the best strategy is to think about ideas in the breaks between other activities and only for a few minutes. This approach will not only make generating ideas fun and easy but will also make your thinking more productive. Remember that you don't need an expensive chair or a fancy office for creating successful business ideas. Your creative studio is wherever you are at the particular moment. Innovative ideas often come in places that you least expect them.

Travel

Many great thinkers have created some of their best business ideas during their travel abroad.

A trip to Denmark inspired Walt Disney to create ideas that he later implemented in Disneyland. Walt wanted Disneyland to have a similar atmosphere of relaxed fun that the Tivoli Gardens amusement park in Copenhagen had.

During his vacation in Jamaica, Richard Branson listened to many local reggae bands. This trip inspired him to create a reggae record label and he signed contracts with over 20 reggae artists.

During his trip to Italy, Howard Schulz noticed that coffee bars existed almost everywhere and not only served excellent espresso, but also served as meeting places for people. Based on his memories of the cafés in Italy, he created Starbucks in the USA that not only served hot coffee but also provided customers with a great experience.

When you travel your brain gets exposed to an environment and experiences that are dramatically different from what you see daily. The dramatic change in surroundings serves as incredibly powerful stimulation for the brain. In fact, it is so powerful that many people say they become more creative not only for the duration of their travel but also for a few more weeks after they arrive home. Whenever you have an opportunity – travel, because travel is one of the most effective creative stimulators in the world.

To make your brain work at maximum capacity, don't let it get too accustomed to your everyday surroundings. Occasionally, change locations where you think: travel to other countries, change locations within a city, move around the office or house. This habit will help you avoid creative blocks and become more effective at producing excellent business ideas.

Mindless activities

Next time when you are bored...

Our brain is an incredibly powerful thinking machine, but when we are busy much of this capacity is unavailable. When we are bored and perform mindless activities, our analytical brain doesn't work and allows the subconscious mind to think at full capacity. Although washing dishes, ironing, jogging on a treadmill or staring at the wall in a subway car doesn't sound inspiring, these activities are very stimulating for creative thinking.

Next time you are bored or need to kill time, instead of listening to an MP3 player, playing games on a mobile phone or reading a book, give your brain a task to think about a particular problem and give your mind a chance to wander. By the time the mindless, repetitive or boring activity is over, you will have generated a lot of interesting ideas. When great thinkers are waiting in line, mowing the lawn or cleaning, they say, "Wow! It's boring. What a fruitful time to think about new ideas."

Idea shower

The executive director of the NeuroLeadership Institute in the U.S., David Rock, polled over 6,000 people to figure out where they generate their best ideas. Guess what? The shower was the most often mentioned location.

Although a shower doesn't look as inspirational as a hammock on the beach at the ocean, it is indeed an incredibly stimulating place for generating ideas. Firstly, a shower is a mindless activity that stimulates daydreaming. Secondly, warm water makes your body relaxed, which is important for high performance of the subconscious mind. Finally, when you go to the shower you change location, which stimulates the brain with a new experience.

Don't waste your shower time! Set tasks for the subconscious and after almost every trip to the shower you will come back with one, two or three good ideas. Make sure to write down all ideas, sometimes even before you finish washing yourself because ideas are the most fragile thing in the world and can evaporate as unexpectedly as they come.

Ideas breed ideas

Ideas stimulate ideas

While talking to an interesting person, listening to a presentation or reading an article, you can often come up with more interesting ideas than during the entire day of sitting at the desk and looking at the wall. Do you know why?

The answer to this question is one of the most important principles of creativity that says: "Ideas stimulate ideas." When you hear or read ideas of other people, they can trigger your brain and inspire you to generate another idea that is either relevant or irrelevant to the topic of the conversation, presentation or article. The more you expose your brain to ideas of other people, the more triggers will be pressed in your brain and the more interesting ideas you will generate.

Great thinkers know this powerful creativity principle and nurture their brains with huge quantities of ideas on a regular basis. They learn the ideas of others that are already successful, ideas that are in the implementation stage and ideas that have just been generated.

If you are working on a problem, expose yourself to external ideas as much as you can. All of them can trigger your brain and stimulate it to look at the problem in a fresh way and generate a successful solution. One of the most effective techniques for stimulating the brain is "ideas bombarding."

Ideas bombarding

This technique will allow you to effectively produce original ideas in a very short period of time. Within 2 hours, look through 100 ideas related to the same task and think about how they can be applied in your existing or future business. Think about how combinations or modifications of these ideas may help you to solve the same task most effectively.

For example, look through websites in your niche to see which ideas you can use on your website. Think about how you can modify these ideas to make them applicable for your business. If you are an author and want to create a title for your book – look through 100 book titles in your genre and see if they can inspire you to create an interesting title for your next book. Write down all the ideas that come to your head during this session.

New ideas are created on top of old ideas. Letting hundreds of ideas through your head will significantly stimulate your right brain to generate successful business ideas within a short period of time. "Ideas bombarding" is one of the most effective creative thinking techniques that exist and it will allow you to generate a lot of excellent ideas, some of which will make your business enormously successful.

Snowball effect

Ideas have a snowballing effect. Once you get any idea, no matter how crazy or unrealistic, further ideas will come faster to your head. As Cliff Einstein, the head of an advertising agency, said, "The best way to get an idea is to get an idea."

Once you think about a task or a problem, the first ideas will come to your head slowly. Then, ideas will come easier and eventually they will come so fast that it will be even difficult to record them. Don't stop this amazing flow of ideas by analyzing or criticizing them. Just appreciate what the subconscious does for you and quickly write down all thoughts and ideas that it generates. You will have plenty of opportunities to analyze and modify them later.

Value and respect all ideas that come to your head. The most crazy and unworkable idea may trigger something in your brain and allow you to come up with a great idea. Remember that there are no bad ideas. There are only successful ideas and ideas that lead us to successful ideas.

When people meet, magic happens

Conversation is a cradle of ideas

During the Age of Enlightenment (17th and 18th centuries) in England, more breakthroughs in art and science were made than during the previous thousand years. Interestingly enough, the beginning of the Age of Enlightenment coincides with the time when coffee was brought to England and coffee houses became popular around the country.

At the beginning of the 17th century, water wasn't safe to drink in England and people had to drink beer or wine for breakfast, lunch and dinner. As you can imagine, the cafés at that time were full of drunk people and weren't suitable for intellectual conversations. After coffee and tea became popular, coffee houses became a place where scientists, artists and great thinkers met and exchanged ideas. These casual conversations often led to breakthroughs in science, literature and art.

Many great ideas are born during your conversation with another person. When your thinking mate hears your raw idea, he or she may share an opinion, hint or thought that can help to make it better. After several rounds of thoughts exchange, your raw idea will evolve, get shaped and become a valuable idea ready for implementation.

Often our subconscious mind generates seeds for the good ideas. Conversation is a soil that allows these seeds to grow into accomplished, high-quality ideas ready for implementation. Many significant advances in business, art and science were made during a casual conversation. Great thinkers often share ideas with other people, because they know that the thoughts exchange significantly improves their creative output.

Innovation comes from people meeting up in the hallways or calling each other at 10:30 at night with a new idea, or because they realized something that shoots holes in how we've been thinking about a problem.
– Steve Jobs

Engage other people to give you ideas

Last year, I launched a contest for the cover design of my book *Magic of Impromptu Speaking* and during the first round received 104 designs from 23 contestants. I showed the top 5 designs to my wife and together we agreed that one of the concepts was significantly stronger than the others. Olena pointed at this design and said, "This cover is great, but it would become stronger with a different background color and slightly changed fonts." I thought that what Olena said made sense and requested a designer to send me several versions of the same cover, however with changes that my wife suggested. One of the covers the designer sent in response became the cover with which the book got published. Many readers sent me emails saying that the cover of *Magic of Impromptu Speaking* is one of the best book covers they have ever seen. Do the readers care that 25 people in total were engaged in developing an idea for the book cover design? No, the only thing they care about is that the cover looks compelling.

You significantly limit your creative potential if you think that all good ideas should be generated, modified and improved only by your own brain. Talk about your problem with other people and use their thoughts, hints and suggestions extensively.

If I didn't engage 24 other people in creating an idea for the *Magic of Impromptu Speaking* book cover, I would not have such a successful design. It's OK that not all of the excellent thoughts popped up in your head, what matters is the end result. Engage as many people in thinking about your tasks as you need and they will increase the quality of your business ideas.

Filtering and executing ideas

3 categories technique

When you have generated and analyzed a significant amount of ideas, you need to select the most promising among them, and the most effective strategy to do so is to use the approach that judges use during castings of the American TV show *So You Think You Can Dance*. If a person danced really well, judges say, "You get a ticket to Las Vegas for the second stage of the selection process." If judges are on the fence, they say, "We invite you to the short test in the afternoon, to see how you can pick up professional choreography." If the dance was clearly bad, the judges say, "You are not ready for this show." This selection process allows judges to select the best dancers out of thousands of candidates within a short period of time.

Imagine that each idea on your list is a candidate and you are a judge. Once you see that an idea is clearly good, mark it with "great idea," if the idea is clearly bad, mark it with "won't fly," and if you are on the fence, mark it with "interesting."

Use your gut feeling and common sense to decide in which category to put each idea. If, for example, you want to introduce a new product to the market, put yourself in your customers' shoes and ask, "Would I buy it?" If you like the product yourself, chances are that many other people will like it, too.

Cross out ideas that "won't fly." Save "interesting ideas" for the future. After further examination and modification you may decide to move them into the "great ideas" category. Move "great ideas" to the next round of the selection process.

Creative buddy

Your creative buddy is the first person with whom you share ideas. A creative buddy can highlight the potential problems in ideas that you haven't noticed as well as suggest how to improve them. Find a person with whom you are on the same wavelength, whom you enjoy being around and whose opinion you trust.

For example when I generate ideas, I first share them with my wife. I know that Olena honestly says if she thinks the idea is good or not and her opinion is always valuable. Time has proven that if Olena approved an idea, the probability that it will become successful is higher.

Your creative buddy can be your better half, friend, colleague or business partner, but most important is that you have an easy rapport with this person and are not afraid to share your silliest ideas. Most people won't be honest with their criticism, but the creative buddy will. Most people won't give you an opinion that you trust, but the creative buddy will. The world's best thinkers know the importance of having a creative buddy and spend years developing relationships with people who they can trust. After your creative buddy has told you that the idea is good, it's worth exposing it to a larger group of people.

Use the opinions of others as additional information for consideration but make a final decision regarding the idea yourself. Remember that there are numerous examples in history where nobody besides the idea creator believed in the idea but eventually it became extraordinarily successful. Once you have made your own analysis and received external opinions, implement your best ideas and let the market say which of them are viable.

Implement ideas with little risk

Take it for granted that no matter how much you analyze an idea and how much feedback you get, it is impossible to predict with 100% probability if it will become successful. Billions of dollars are lost every year by companies who invest in ideas that sound great on paper but, once faced with the real world, fail due to various reasons.

Great thinkers know, "Only the market can make the final decision of whether the idea is viable. The best way to see if an idea is worth significant investment of time and money is to implement it with little risk."

Imagine that you own an international chain of restaurants and want to introduce a new snack to the menu. Introduce it first in a single restaurant or a single city. If the snack proves to be popular, invest in introducing it on a larger scale; if not, you haven't lost a lot of time and money. By testing your ideas before implementing them on a large scale, you minimize the losses in case of failure.

At the international design firm IDEO the employees do frequent and quick prototyping for product ideas. At Pixar, animators show their work in early stages to the entire animation crew. Test your ideas on a small scale and let unsuccessful ones fail as soon as possible to minimize your expenses and time loss. If the idea doesn't fail at the test stage, invest more money and time into it because, most likely, it is one of those ideas that will make your company highly successful.

Implement your best ideas with a small investment of time and money and let the market decide which of them will survive. Immediately discard ideas that failed during the test stage and invest in those that worked. This strategy will allow you to build a profitable business with minimum risk.

Failures are an essential part of the creative process and the greater the number of your ideas that fail, the more will eventually succeed. The world's most successful thinkers have more failures than other people but they are small and affordable.

"100, 20, 5, 1" rule

Once you have generated hundreds of ideas you may ask, "How can I figure out which of them will become successful?" The "100, 20, 5, 1" rule says that after going through the list of 100 ideas, you reduce it to the 20 most promising ones on your own. After asking for the opinion of your creative buddy and the small group of potential customers, you further reduce the list to 5 ideas worth implementing. After implementing 5 ideas, 4 of them either fail or give mediocre results but 1 becomes incredibly successful. Of course 100, 20, 5, 1 are only ballpark figures, but they give a good estimate of what it takes to get one idea that will make a significant positive impact on your business.

Some of the greatest ideas in business history were selected using the "100, 20, 5, 1" rule.

Endure opposition and frustrations

Great ideas face opposition

When we create great ideas we expect people to say, "Wow! What a great idea! I can't wait to buy your products and services." However, very often even the most successful business projects in the world such as the telephone, radio and The Beatles band initially receive negative feedback and face opposition.

Associates of David Sarnoff replied to his request to invest in radio in 1921: "The wireless music box has no imaginable commercial value. Who would pay for a message sent to no one in particular?"

After the audition by The Beatles, the Decca Records executive gave his verdict to the band's manager: "Not to mince words, Mr. Epstein, but we don't like your boys' sound. Groups are out; four-piece groups with guitars particularly are finished."

Western Union officials who reviewed Alexander Graham Bell's offer to purchase his telephone patent wrote: "The Telephone purports to transmit the speaking voice over telegraph wires. We found that the voice is very weak and indistinct, and grows even weaker when long wires are used between the transmitter and receiver. Technically, we do not see that this device will ever be capable of sending recognizable speech over a distance of several miles. Messer Hubbard and Bell want to install one of their 'telephone devices' in every city. The idea is idiotic on the face of it. Furthermore, why would any person want to use this ungainly and impractical device when he can send a messenger to the telegraph office and have a clear written message sent to any large city in the United States?"

You might ask, "Why does it happen?" Well, there are 3 major reasons why people say "It won't work" even to the world's greatest ideas:

Firstly, people are often averse to the unknown and, just like David Sarnoff's associates, don't realize the potential of the product before they have seen, tested or used it. Once you have implemented an idea and received positive feedback from your first customers, the same people will say that your idea is great.

Secondly, many people are too concentrated on their past experience and make predictions about the future based on what worked in the past. For example, the Decca Records executive knew many four-piece bands that were not popular and after seeing that The Beatles band consisted of four musicians made a prediction that it would fail.

Finally, many people tend to concentrate on why the idea won't work rather than how to make it work or what potential it may have. Just like with the idea of the telephone, it is possible to find plenty of reasons "Why it won't work" for almost any idea. That's why even most successful ideas in the world initially faced opposition.

Use feedback from people you share ideas with as additional information for consideration but remember that even the world's best ideas initially faced opposition. If you believe in an idea, implement it no matter what everyone else is saying so you don't regret your entire life that you didn't.

It's really hard to design products by focus groups. A lot of times, people don't know what they want until you show it to them. — Steve Jobs

If you have a good idea, 99 percent of people will tell you why it's not good or how it's been done before or why else you're going to fall flat on your face. You've just got to say, "Screw it, just do it" and get on with it. — Richard Branson

It's very difficult for people when they're doing their own thing to do it their own way entirely, not taking notes from anyone else, not taking anyone else's advice. Do it the way you want to do it, don't listen to other people. — James Dyson

Be persistent. Creative thinking is a marathon

In 1979 James Dyson bought one of the most advanced vacuum cleaners on the market, and after using it got frustrated with how quickly it clogged and began losing suction. James got excited about this problem and decided, "I will design a vacuum cleaner that will clean the house more effectively."

Partly supported by the salary of his wife, who worked as an art teacher, and partly by bank loans, James spent almost 5 years working on his vacuum cleaner design and after 5,126 failed prototypes eventually created a working version of a dual-cyclone bagless vacuum cleaner.

James realized that no company in the UK wanted to buy his technology or collaborate in manufacturing his vacuum cleaner, and retailers were reluctant to sell the product of an unknown brand. After generating many more interesting business ideas about how to overcome these obstacles, James first launched his vacuum cleaner through catalogue sales in Japan where it became incredibly successful. In a few years, the Dyson vacuum cleaner became one of the most desirable household appliances worldwide and James Dyson became a billionaire.

In an interview with Forbes magazine, James was asked if he ever wanted to give up. And here is what he replied: "I wanted to give up almost every day. But one of the things I did when I was young was long distance running, from a mile up to ten miles. They wouldn't let me run more than ten miles at school – in those days they thought you'd drop down dead or something. And I was quite good at it, not because I was physically good, but because I had more determination. I learned determination from it.

"More particularly, I learned that the moment you want to slow down is the moment you should accelerate. In long distance running, you go through a pain barrier. The same thing happens in research and development projects, or in starting any business. There's a terrible moment when failure is staring you in the face. And actually if you persevere a bit longer you'll start to climb out of it."

Of course in the majority of cases great thinkers don't encounter as many failures and difficulties as James Dyson did but they are all creative "long distance" runners. If you say to yourself, "I am in business for a long time, I am ready to endure frustrations and persist in creating and testing ideas on the way to achieving my dream," you are destined to have enormous success.

Success is a lousy teacher. It seduces smart people into thinking they can't lose. — *Bill Gates*

Creativity habit

Train creative muscles

In 7th grade, my math teacher Alexander said to my mother, "Victoria, your son's performance is very poor. Honestly, I think math isn't his thing. It would be better for Andrii if you transfer him to another school at the end of the year." My classmate Peter was a naturally gifted student and several heads above everyone I knew at math. He always solved problems nobody else could and Alexander called him "math heavy artillery."

In 8th grade, after one incident in class I became very interested in math. I began devoting all my spare time to math and by the end of the year became the second-best math student in the class after Peter. In 9th grade, Peter became very interested in guitar, founded his own band and neglected math. By the end of the 9th grade, I outperformed Peter and became the strongest math student in the entire school. In 10th grade, I continued devoting at least 4 hours a day to solving problems and by the end of the year became one of the 100 best math students in the Ukraine.

Peter is certainly much more gifted than I am, but I trained significantly more. I am sure that if he devoted at least half the time that I did to math he would achieve far better results than I. If you are interested to know what happened to Peter later, he became a guitar player in one of the most popular bands in the Ukraine.

When a person finishes a marathon in under 3 hours we don't say, "Wow, he is a running genius," we say, "He or she trained a lot. Anybody can run a marathon in under 3 hours after a couple of years of daily training."

However, when talking about the world's best thinkers, people often say, "They are geniuses. I will never be able to create such awesome ideas." Guess what? The world's best thinkers are able to generate successful ideas not because they are geniuses, but because they think about ideas daily and have trained their creative muscles more than other people. If you practice generating ideas regularly, after some time you will produce better ideas than the majority of naturally gifted people, because your creative muscles will be stronger.

Any person who trained for a marathon for several years would outperform a gifted runner who didn't. Any person who practices creativity daily will outperform at creating successful business ideas any genius who doesn't.

The more you practice pushups, the more pushups you will be able to do. The same happens with ideas. The more you practice creative thinking, the quicker high-quality ideas will come to your head. If you take practicing ideas generation seriously, in a few years other people may call you a creative genius.

The majority of people rarely give tasks to their subconscious and once they see that their creative muscles are weak say, "I am just not a creative type." It sounds the same as, "I exercise only twice a year and can't do more than 5 pushups. I don't have the talent for pushups."

Fortune top-15 writers write about 5 novels a year. How can they be that productive? They write daily and their writing muscles are very strong. If you want to become world-class at generating business ideas, you need to exercise your creative muscles regularly. If you think about ideas daily, you will generate better ideas than naturally gifted people who don't.

Certainly, every child is born blessed with a vivid imagination. But just as muscles grow flabby with disuse, so the bright imagination of a child pales in later years if he ceases to exercise it. – Walt Disney

Develop a creativity habit

Anders Ericsson studied young violinists and pianists in their early twenties at the Music Academy of West Berlin. He asked music professors to split students into 3 groups: exceptional students most likely to become international solo performers, very good students most likely to join the world's best orchestras and least able students most likely to become music teachers.

Ericsson discovered that students in all groups had remarkably similar backgrounds and the only difference between them was the amount of practice time. By the age of 20, exceptional students had practiced on average 10,000 hours; good pianists and violinists 8,000 hours and those most likely to become music teachers 4,000 hours.

Everybody who was in the elite group of top musicians had spent on average 10,000 hours practicing during their lifetime and everybody who had spent at least 10,000 hours practicing was in the elite group of top musicians. Further research of top chess players, dancers, salespeople and scientists confirmed that the amount of practice rather than talent makes a person an expert in his or her domain. Ericsson wrote, "The differences between expert performers and normal adults reflect a life-long persistence of deliberate effort to improve performance."

The same is true in creativity. The more experience you have in creating ideas, the faster your brain will make connections and generate successful business ideas. To become an exceptional thinker you need to develop a habit of thinking about ideas daily.

Practicing ideas generation is easier than playing chess, violin or piano because the majority of thinking is done by the creative brain while you are not consciously thinking. However, to activate your creative brain you need to think about ideas that can improve your life regularly for at least 15 minutes.

The more you practice thinking creatively, the less time it will take to come up with a great business idea and the more you will enjoy the process. After some time you will become a world-class thinker and exceptional ideas will come to your head in abundance.

Final checklist

To significantly increase the quantity and quality of ideas that you generate, reading this book isn't enough. You need to make principles from this book a part of your own habits.

Below you will find the 7 most fundamental principles of creating successful business ideas. Write them down on a sheet of paper and hang it near the desk where you work or near your bed. Over the next 3 weeks, think for at least 15-30 minutes per day about ideas using these principles. These can be ideas that will help you improve your business, achieve your dreams or make your life more interesting. I promise you that by the end of these 3 weeks you will notice a significant jump in your creative performance.

1. **Collect raw materials.** Ideas are combinations or modifications of other ideas. The more you know the ideas of other people and the more life experiences you expose yourself to, the more creative raw materials you have. The more creative raw materials you have, the more combinations your subconscious mind will be able to make and the more likely you are to create new valuable and interesting ideas.

2. **Set the task for the subconscious mind.** Your subconscious mind is a powerful thinking mechanism, but it remains idle if you haven't given it a task. Once you begin giving your subconscious questions to think about regularly, you will notice how the quantity and quality of your ideas will skyrocket.

3. **Separate analyzing and generating ideas.** When you are analyzing ideas, your analytical brain blocks your superfast

creative brain from thinking. To let the creative brain do its work, separate the processes of analyzing and generating ideas.

4. **Think and rest.** The most effective thinking algorithm is the following: think about a problem for an extensive period of time, forget about the problem and rest, occasionally think about the problem for few minutes and forget about it again. The incubation period when you don't think about the problem is essential for your subconscious mind to process millions of thoughts and combinations of ideas, however to give it a task you need to think for some time about the problem consciously.

5. **Generate many ideas.** In creative thinking, quantity equals quality. You can't generate one great idea. However, you can generate many ideas and select one or several great ideas out of them.

6. **Have fun.** Your subconscious mind thinks most effectively when you have fun. When you are serious, you are very unlikely to create really creative and valuable ideas.

7. **Believe and desire.** Believe that you will generate great ideas and have a burning desire to generate them. If you do, great ideas will come to you in abundance and sooner or later the problem will be solved.

Once you have made these 7 principles a part of your own creative habits, glance through the book again and practice other principles and techniques. In a year's time of practicing generating ideas regularly, you will become a world-class creative thinker. The skill of creating ideas will make your business successful and your life an adventure. I wish you good luck in creating successful ideas and in achieving all your dreams in business.

What to read next?

If you liked this book, you will also like *The Millionaire Factory: A Complete System for Becoming Insanely Rich.* The Millionaire Factory is a comprehensive system aimed to guide people with any talent, personality and occupation to become insanely rich.

Another interesting book is *Magic of Impromptu Speaking: Create a Speech That Will Be Remembered for Years in Under 30 Seconds.* In this book, you will learn how to be in the moment, speak without preparation and always find the right words when you need them.

I also highly recommend you to read *Magic of Public Speaking: A Complete System to Become a World Class Speaker.* By using this system, you can unleash your public speaking potential in a very short period of time.

Biography

At the age of 19, Andrii obtained his CCIE (Certified Cisco Internetwork Expert) certification, the most respected certification in the IT world, and became the youngest person in Europe to hold it.

At the age of 23, he joined an MBA program at one of the top 10 MBA schools in the USA as the youngest student in the program, and at the age of 25 he joined Cisco Systems' Head Office as a Product Manager responsible for managing a router which brought in $1 billion in revenue every year.

These and other experiences have taught Andrii that success in any endeavor doesn't as much depend on the amount of experience you have but rather on the processes that you are using. Having dedicated over 10 years to researching behavior of world's most successful people and testing a variety of different techniques, Andrii has uncovered principles that will help you to unleash your potential and fulfill your dreams in a very short period of time.

The Millionaire Factory
A Complete System for Becoming Insanely Rich

The Millionaire Factory is a comprehensive system aimed to guide people with any talent, personality and occupation to become insanely rich. It is based on 10 years of research of billionaires, serial entrepreneurs, Wall Street investors and highly paid employees. The book is entertaining to read and includes many insights backed up by scientific research and real-life examples of how to maximize your primary source of income and invest money with highest return. The concepts of the system are aimed at changing your financial mindset, revealing secrets of the richest people in the world and tuning your internal money magnet to work at full capacity.

Magic of Impromptu Speaking

Create a Speech That Will Be Remembered for Years in Under 30 Seconds

Magic of Impromptu Speaking is a comprehensive, step-by-step system for creating highly effective speeches in under 30 seconds. It is based on research of the most powerful techniques used by winners of impromptu speaking contests, politicians, actors and successful presenters. The book is entertaining to read, has plenty of examples and covers the most effective tools not only from the world of impromptu speaking but also from acting, stand-up comedy, applied psychology and creative thinking.

Once you master the system, you will grow immensely as an impromptu public speaker, become a better storyteller in a circle of friends and be more creative in everyday life. Your audience members will think that what you do on stage after such short preparation is pure magic and will recall some of your speeches many years later.

Magic of Public Speaking

A Complete System to Become a World Class Speaker

The Magic of Public Speaking is a comprehensive step-by-step system for creating highly effective speeches. It is based on research from the top 1000 speakers in the modern world. The techniques you will learn have been tested on hundreds of professional speakers and work! You will receive the exact steps needed to create a speech that will keep your audience on the edge of their seats. The book is easy to follow, entertaining to read and uses many examples from real speeches. This system will make sure that every time you go on stage your speech is an outstanding one.

CPSIA information can be obtained
at www.ICGtesting.com
Printed in the USA
LVHW021749230720
661378LV00018B/1825

9 781074 384111